LAWS OF SPIRITUAL LEADERSHIP

LEADING GOD'S PEOPLE

BOOK 8

ZACHARIAS TANEE FOMUM

Published by

*A division of the Book Ministry of Christian
Missionary Fellowship International*

info@books4revival.com

CONTENTS

PREFACE

The content of this book, *Laws of Spiritual Leadership* were first delivered to the saints in the church in Yaounde in 2005 by the author, Professor Z.T. Fomum, during her weekly leadership training sessions.

The messages carry a strong voice of Scripture on <u>simple down to earth godly leadership principles</u>, with examples from both the Old and New Testaments. Both the aspiring as well as those already involved in Christian leadership will find their lot.

The leader must set and maintain a leadership gap between himself and those he is leading. The author suggests twelve such domains in which the potential leader should seek and establish distinction. For, no one can honestly lead from behind. You cannot lead those who are ahead of you in the knowledge and pursuit of God. Never! <u>Leadership is a call to give God to the people</u>.

In this book, you will also learn <u>why God chooses certain people</u>, as well as <u>the kind of people He chooses for leadership</u>—the choice of leadership being His sole prerogative.

We send this book out persuaded that the Lord would be glad to use it to raise worthy and competent leaders for His people.

LEADERSHIP GAP BY MIGHT AND DEEDS OF MIGHT

There must be the leader's gap

Tuesday, 11th October, 2005.

The First Law of Spiritual Leadership that I want us to consider today: There must be the Leader's Gap. People cannot be at the same level and talk about leadership. The leader is ahead so that the people follow. The leader is ahead so that all who are honest can follow him. There must be the leader's gap. He must be obviously ahead of the people he is leading. He must be obviously ahead of the people he is leading so that they see him ahead and follow him.

How can people follow a person who is behind? They have to turn about and then follow him in the wrong direction.

Let us read from the Scriptures. Let's take the example of **Saul**, the first king of Israel,

There was a Benjamite, a man of standing, whose name was Kish son of Abiel, the son of Zeror, the son of Becorath, the son of Aphiah

of Benjamin. He had a son named Saul, an impressive young man without equal among the Israelites--a head taller than any of the others (1 Samuel 9:1-2).

"Without equal among the Israelites - a head taller than any of the others" – He had the leadership gap without equal, without equal. Impressive. Without equal among the Israelites, a head taller than any of the Israelites.

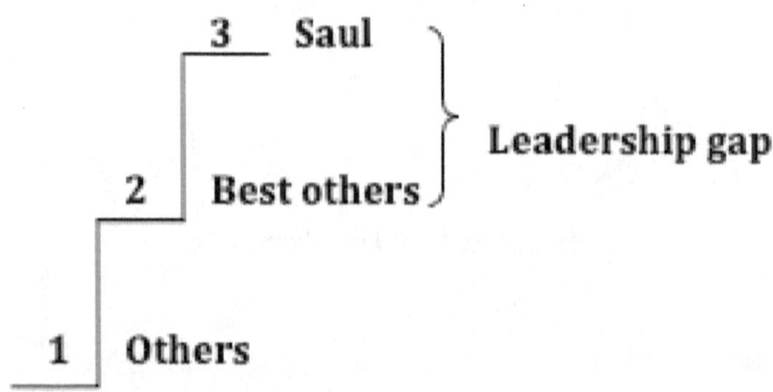

The "Best others" were there at position 2; O, but Saul was at 3. There must be a gap. There must be a gap. The others – 1, the "Best others" – 2. And Saul was at three. That's the leadership gap – the difference between 2 and 3. If you try to lead your equal, you are dishonest.

So they inquired further of the LORD, "Has the man come here yet?" And the LORD said, "Yes, he has hidden himself among the baggage." They ran and brought him out, and as he stood among the people he was a head taller than any of the others. Samuel said to all the people, "Do you see the man the LORD has chosen? There is no one like him among all the people." Then the people shouted, "Long live the king!" (1 Samuel 10:22-24)

They ran and brought him out, and as he stood among the people he was a head taller than any of the others. Samuel said to all the people, 'Do you see the man the LORD has chosen? There is no one like him among all the people.'

Then the people shouted, 'Long live the king!'"

He must be ahead of the people, ahead of the people. The people were compelled by the evidence to shout, "Long live the king!" He was a head taller than any of the others.

Let's come to **DAVID**.

> *So Saul said to his attendants, "Find someone who plays well and bring him to me." One of the servants answered, "I have seen a son of Jesse of Bethlehem who knows how to play the harp. He is a brave man and a warrior. He speaks well and is a fine-looking man. And the LORD is with him"* (1 Samuel 16:17-18).

1. He knows how to play the harp.
2. He is a brave man.
3. A warrior.
4. He speaks well.
5. He's fine-looking.
6. And the Lord is with him

He brought a six-point superiority record into leadership. And he knew it. He was that and he knew it. When a question was asked as to whether David could confront Goliath,

In 1Samuel 17:32-37,

> *David said to Saul, "Let no one lose heart on account of this Philistine; your servant will go and fight him." Saul replied, "You are not able to go out against this Philistine and fight him; you are only a boy, and he has been a fighting man from his youth." But David said*

to Saul, "Your servant has been keeping his father's sheep. When a lion or a bear came and carried off a sheep from the flock, I went after it, struck it and rescued the sheep from its mouth. When it turned on me, I seized it by its hair, struck it and killed it. Your servant has killed both the lion and the bear; this uncircumcised Philistine will be like one of them, because he has defied the armies of the living God. The LORD who delivered me from the paw of the lion and the paw of the bear will deliver me from the hand of this Philistine." Saul said to David, "Go, and the LORD be with you."

There must be unchallengeable superiority. The people must know it and the leader must know it. Part of the confidence for his leadership is the fact that at the human level no one can do it better than him. He is not perfect but he's better than all the rest.

To attempt to lead people who are better than you is dishonest. And you can go on to narrate how he won one victory after another.

About **SOLOMON**.

God gave Solomon wisdom and very great insight, and a breadth of understanding as measureless as the sand on the seashore. Solomon's wisdom was greater than the wisdom of all the men of the East, and greater than all the wisdom of Egypt. He was wiser than any other man, including Ethan the Ezrahite--wiser than Heman, Calcol and Darda, the sons of Mahol. And his fame spread to all the surrounding nations. He spoke three thousand proverbs and his songs numbered a thousand and five. He described plant life, from the cedar of Lebanon to the hyssop that grows out of walls. He also taught about animals and birds, reptiles and fish. Men of all nations came to listen to Solomon's wisdom, sent by all the kings of the world, who had heard of his wisdom (1 Kings 4:29-34).

Come with me to Exodus 31. You see, each time God chooses a leader, he's a way ahead. Men can choose what they want but when God chooses a leader, He is choosing him for a gap.

Then the LORD said to Moses, See, I have chosen Bezalel son of Uri, the son of Hur, of the tribe of Judah, and I have filled him with the Spirit of God, with skill, ability and knowledge in all kinds of crafts--to make artistic designs for work in gold, silver and bronze, to cut and set stones, to work in wood, and to engage in all kinds of craftsmanship. Moreover, I have appointed Oholiab son of Ahisamach, of the tribe of Dan, to help him. Also I have given skill to all the craftsmen to make everything I have commanded you (Exodus 31:1- 6)

There's another passage about **Bezalel**.

Then Moses said to the Israelites, "See, the LORD has chosen Bezalel son of Uri, the son of Hur, of the tribe of Judah, and he has filled him with the Spirit of God, with skill, ability and knowledge in all kinds of crafts--to make artistic designs for work in gold, silver and bronze, to cut and set stones, to work in wood and to engage in all kinds of artistic craftsmanship. And he has given both him and Oholiab son of Ahisamach, of the tribe of Dan, the ability to teach others. He has filled them with skill to do all kinds of work as crafts-men, designers, embroiderers in blue, purple and scarlet yarn and fine linen, and weavers--all of them master craftsmen and designers (Exodus 35:30-35).

I am awed; it frightens me - the superiority of Bezalel. It's as if he could do everything.

Look at the leadership of **Peter:**

Nevertheless, more and more men and women believed in the Lord and were added to their number. As a result, people brought the sick into the streets and laid them on beds and mats so that at least Peter's shadow might fall on some of them as he passed by. Crowds gathered also from the towns around Jerusalem, bringing their sick and those tormented by evil spirits, and all of them were healed (Acts 5:14-16).

The shadow of Peter could heal. Later on, in Acts 9: 32-35:

As Peter traveled about the country, he went to visit the saints in Lydda. There he found a man named Aeneas, a paralytic who had been bedridden for eight years. Aeneas, Peter said to him, "Jesus Christ heals you. Get up and take care of your mat." Immediately Aeneas got up. All those who lived in Lydda and Sharon saw him and turned to the Lord.

Then Dorcas died.

Acts 9:39-42:

Peter went with them, and when he arrived he was taken upstairs to the room. All the widows stood around him, crying and showing him the robes and other clothing that Dorcas had made while she was still with them. Peter sent them all out of the room; then he got down on his knees and prayed. Turning toward the dead woman, he said, "Tabitha, get up." She opened her eyes, and seeing Peter she sat up. He took her by the hand and helped her to her feet. Then he called the believers and the widows and presented her to them alive. This became known all over Joppa, and many people believed in the Lord.

He was just ahead.

Paul

2 Corinthians 11:21-27:

To my shame I admit that we were too weak for that! What anyone else dares to boast about--I am speaking as a fool--I also dare to boast about. Are they Hebrews? So am I. Are they Israelites? So am I. Are they Abraham's descendants? So am I. Are they servants of Christ? (I am out of my mind to talk like this.) I am more. I have worked much harder, been in prison more frequently, been flogged more severely, and been exposed to death again and again. Five times I received from the Jews the forty lashes minus one. Three times I was beaten with rods, once I was stoned, three times I was ship-wrecked, I spent a night and a day in the open sea, I have been constantly on the move. I have been in danger from rivers, in danger from bandits, in danger from my own countrymen, in danger from Gentiles; in danger in the city, in danger in the country, in danger at sea; and in danger from false brothers. I have labored and toiled and have often gone without sleep; I have known hunger and thirst and have often gone without food; I have been cold and naked.

Much harder, more, more, more, more, more, suffered, suffered, suffered, suffered, suffered.

And listen, brethren, it is not tied to wearing trousers.

In Judges 4:4,

Deborah, a prophetess, the wife of Lappidoth, was leading Israel at that time.

In fact, since she was a woman and she could not lead the people to war,

Barak said to her, 'If you go with me, I will go; but if you don't go with me, I won't go." 'Very well,' Deborah said, 'I will go with you' (Judges 4 : 8 - 9a).

She was the authority. She was the leader.

But in order that you may not misunderstand, come with me to Acts 14. Saul of Tarsus with Barnabas went on a missionary journey, evangelising and planting churches. They were in some places for very short periods. On their return journey – some Bible scholars say that that first missionary journey lasted eighteen months – they preached the gospel and planted churches. In Acts 14:23,

> *Paul and Barnabas appointed elders for them in each church and, with prayer and fasting, committed them to the Lord, in whom they had put their trust.*

These converts, the oldest of them was one-and-a-half years, but they were ahead of the others. They chose those who were ahead. They chose those who were ahead and made them Elders. They were ahead of others. They were very, very young still but they were ahead of others so that the others could follow.

In Primary School, even though people are young and inexperienced, there are leaders. Leaders are appointed. Why is everybody not appointed? Not everybody is ahead. Normally, the person who is ahead is appointed the leader. The question is: Is the person ahead of the others? He may not be perfect, he may never be perfect; but is he ahead of the others?

On the mission field, we ordain Elders who would not be Deacons at all, at all if they were in Yaounde; but they are ahead of the others.

You may ask the question: "In what should I be ahead?"

Let me give you twelve things:

1. Praying Alone
2. Daily Dynamic Encounters with God
3. Bible Reading
4. Reading of Christian Literature
5. Fasting
6. Giving to God
7. Praying with Others
8. Being a Disciple of the Lord Jesus
9. Soul-winning
10. The Making of Disciples for Jesus Christ
11. Being an Active Member of the Local Church
12. Accountability

If you want to be a leader someday, those are the basic things of the christian life. Excel in them.

That's where we stop teaching on this principle of the leader's gap and the need for it.

I was showing the brethren a copy of *Cameroon Tribune* of 1978. We were on the first page and we were on the fifth page. It was a report of the Bamenda Crusade for Christ which we held then. On my way to the Crusade, I left brother J. M. in charge of the small flock that was in Yaounde then. He was only six to seven months old in the Lord, but he was ahead of the others. So I made him pastor and he's been pastor in increasing depth, height, girth and so on until today. I didn't go and hire somebody of five years from India or from Japan. He was ahead of the others though less than one year old. He was made the leader.

The leader is ahead. People follow the one who is ahead. And you know, even Jesus was rejected, but He was not always rejected.

If you are a young believer, set your mind to be a leader someday and put in everything to grow rapidly and become a leader.

Let me tell you that I set out a thirty-six-point leadership strategy. I'm called to lead beyond the nation and beyond the continent. I asked the question: "What will make them follow me wherever I go?" I have not dealt with the inner qualities. Those will come up someday.

HOMEWORK:

For those who are already leaders:

- What are the areas in which you are ahead of the people you are leading?
- And in what areas must you work on in order to honestly maintain your place as leader?

Brethren, this principle made me understand so many things. I now understood John Wesley. I now understood Goforth. I now understand Watchman Nee. I understand C. T. Studd. When you abandon paying the price, you also abandon leadership. When you drop, you have forsaken leadership. But you can stay on like Saul did while leadership has passed into the hands of another.

THE PRICE PAID FOR LEADERSHIP MUST BE MAINTAINED AND INCREASED

Tuesday, 18th October, 2005

Last week, we had our first lesson on Spiritual Leadership. We said the leader must be far above the people he leads. He must be far above the people he leads; if not, he has abandoned leadership. We saw very clearly that God chooses people who are outstanding, mighty, people very far ahead of others and places them to lead. Today we want to look at the second lesson.

The second lesson is that the price that was paid earlier to attain leadership must be maintained in order to conserve leadership. The price that was paid to ascend to leadership must continue to be paid in order that leadership is maintained. We say it again: The price that was paid to ascend to leadership must continue to be paid and increased to if leadership is to be maintained.

If a man was praying for two hours a day before he became a leader, and does not now pray three, four, five hours, he has abandoned leadership. God will remove him! If he was reading his Bible once a year before, but does not now read it two, three, four times, God will remove him! If he was taking one long fast a year and he does not now do two or three, God will remove him! If he was giving sacrificially to God and he is not giving more sacrificially as leader, God will remove him! If he hated sin and he does not hate sin even more, God will remove him. If he was separated from the love of the world and he is not even more separated from the love of the world, God will remove him! If he was separated from the love of the things of the world and he is not even more separated from the love of the things that are in the world, God will remove him! If he spent five hours with God and he is not now spending more than five hours with God, God will remove him. If he was investing seven hours a day in the work of the Lord and he is not investing seven plus more hours in the service of the Lord, God will remove him! He cannot turn from the pursuit of God to the pursuit of his family and maintain his leadership! He cannot turn from the pursuit of God to the pursuit of the safety of his children and maintain his leadership! Leadership is maintained by ever-increasing sacrifice for the Lord and for the Lord's interest. Leadership is maintained by ever-increasing sacrifice for the Lord and for the work of the Lord. Leadership is maintained by ever-increasing risks taken for the Lord and for the interests of the Lord. Leadership is maintained by rising to ever-increasing vision for the Lord and for His interests. In maintaining leadership, there are two aspects. There is the aspect of being and the aspect of doing - the aspect of "Before God" and "Before Man."

The person who will maintain his leadership must grow in faith, must grow in discipline, must grow in suffering, must grow in sacrifice. He must grow in the discipline of his body. He must grow in the buffeting of his body.

The Apostle Paul says,

> *No, I beat my body and make it my slave so that after I have preached to others, I myself will not be disqualified for the prize* (1 Corinthians 9:27).

He must not only be ahead at the time of his appointment; he must continue to be ahead, he must continue to run faster than others, suffering more than others, putting in more time than others, denying himself more than others, despising the world more than others, considering the offers of the world as rubbish more than others. There must be ever-increasing depth—ever-increasing depth in the Lord, ever-increasing length in the Lord, ever-increasing width, ever-increasing heights, if he would maintain his leadership, lest God remove him.

I just want to say this: If he does not spend ever-increasing time with God, he is done for. He has committed spiritual suicide. I just want to tell you, brother: If you are not spending more time with God now than you did in the past, God will remove you. There is no time now to talk about the ways by which God removes a man. But God will not keep a man who is joking with leadership! God will not maintain in leadership a man whose vision of God is not becoming sharper, taller and more captivating. A man who is not spending more and more time with God is already out. It's only a matter of time because leadership is a call to gaze into the face of God. It is a call to love God with all one's heart, with all one's strength, with all one's might. It is a call to invest everything into the love of God, the knowledge of God. It is God! God! God! God! God! Leadership is a call to divine fusion, to fusion with God.

And that fusion cannot be had while flirting with men; rather, it is by the being before God. It's just first of all a matter of time. You have God to the extent that you spend time alone with Him. You have God to the extent that you spend time with Him alone. God is imparted to you in the secrecy of your time in His presence alone. So this growth in God content is determinant.

I was touched two days ago by what is said in the Sermon on the Mount.

It's found in Matthew 6:6a

> *But when you pray, go into your room, close the door and pray to your Father, who is unseen.*

Who is unseen – your room, your door, your Father; there's nothing of another person there. That's where everything is determined. It is there that the "shekina" glory comes upon the leader. And in the power of that glory he maintains a leadership that satisfies the heart of God. So if there is not increasing time with God alone, he has abandoned leadership. And God will remove him by any means because it is the God-content of a man that makes a man a leader. And it is the God-content that keeps a man in leadership. When the God-content declines, the man is no longer a leader. He can stand before men, but God is planning to remove him because the man who stands before men in God's Name must know God more than the people before whom he stands. His content of God must be far more than theirs. God must continue to say, "This is the leader." God must continue to say, "There is no one here like this man." If God does not say that about the leader, he is no longer leading before God. The God-content! The God-content! The God-content! The God-content! The God-content! The God-content! The God-content! It is the God-content that makes a man to be made a leader by God. And when that content declines, he has walked off from the stage even if people keep him there. I want to say and say emphatically: It is the God-content that qualifies a man to stand before men. And as he increases that God-content, he rises. As he increases that God-content, he rises. When the God-content drops, it is "Adieu." It is "Good-bye" from leadership. Pray that this would be understood. There is no way to run away from it.

I want just to speak a word to the wives here. If your husband is spending less time before God alone than he did in the past, if you don't do anything to arrest the situation, you would be in for the worst because when a man backslides before God he can still be an activist before men. Whether he's an apostle, a prophet, an evangelist, a pastor or a teacher he must be a man of God's presence. The apostle is called to a different Ministry from that of a prophet, that of an evangelist, that of a pastor-teacher. There will be diversities of Ministries, but the God-content! The God-content! Oh the God-content! The God-content! O, the time before God alone! The time before God alone! The time before God alone! The time before God alone! O, the time before God alone! If it's not increasing, it's doom - because it is the hypocrisy of trying to give men what the man doesn't have or the hypocrisy of trying to give men what he no longer has, the hypocrisy of standing before men when one has not stood before God, the hypocrisy of standing before men more than one stands before God. Running here and there, touching this, spending time before men may be the spirit of an activist. If it does not overflow from an abundant and ever-increasing time in union with God, folly has been committed.

To maintain your leadership, you maintain and add to your God-content. You spend more time with God alone because all things are sorted out there. There are many people who tell you, "I am twenty years in the Lord," but they backslid five years ago or they backslid after one year. These years do not mean a thing.

The leader who wants to maintain his leadership has only one gaze - the gaze at God. He comes to the people only when he is overflowing with God. Like a nursing mother, you know sometimes the breast gets full of milk, so the baby has to suck for the mother to be comfortable. That is the condition for ministry. There is so much so that some must go away for you to be comfortable because leadership is a call to minister from the overflow of abundance. It is the call to minister from the overflow of spiritual wealth. It is the call to minister from overflowing spiritual wealth.

I want you to take it with utter seriousness: Ninety percent of the leaders in the Bible ended at the bottom. They were no longer leaders before God in the end. O, they lost the pursuit of God! They lost the pursuit of God! They lost the glory of God. They lost the wealth that comes from dwelling in God. They continued to be acting before men and it brought about utter shame.

Look at just your Prayer Alone. If you are where you were five years ago, you have resigned from leadership - your Bible Reading, your reading of Christian Literature, your Daily Dynamic Encounters With God, your Giving to God, your Fasting life, and many of these things that can only really be done alone, those things that keep you alone in the presence of God. If there is not a continuing increase, you have abandoned leadership. You are now an actor.

There is only one reason why people don't spend time with God. It's not the shortage of time. It is a shortage of the hunger for God. The heart has gone dull and cold. The fire has gone out. If a man says, "I'm not spending much time with God because I'm busy," he's a crook. He's not spending time alone with God because he doesn't want it. God is not his joy. God is not his joy. God is not his fulfilment. God is not his supreme attraction. Something of God wars against him. So it can't be a matter of little time available. It's a matter of the disposition of the heart. If the heart is right, if he has six hours, he will give five to God and God will multiply that one hour for the service of others six times.

It's just like the leader's Giving. When a man drops in his Giving, he has resigned. God will remove him. He has said that something else is better than building the Kingdom of God. Because money is directional, when a man drops in his Giving, he sinks — no question about it, no, no question about it. There is no question about it! There is no question about it! Nobody has ever decided to give God less and risen spiritually - never, never, never; never, never, never; never, never, never, never, never, never; never, never. Just as sure as there is the living God, just as sure as there is the living God, no one has ever decided to decrease what he gives to God in order to meet his interests without falling off. It's a law. When new needs arise and new challenges arise, the man whose heart is correct gives more to God and then God multiples what is left a thousand fold. And this is the grave of people. If someone was giving God 60% and that 60% represented 60,000 (francs), now he has new responsibilities. So if he gave God 60%, it meant that he had 40,000 for himself.

70%   70,000

60%   ~~60,000~~

Now he has new challenges that demand that he now needs 60,000. Two pathways are open He can reduce God's portion to 40,000 in order to have the 60,000. When he does that, everything will drop—His God-content will drop, his hunger for God will drop, his seeking God will drop. Everything will drop because he has exalted the needs of man above the needs of God. And problems will come from left and right, forward and backward because he has not believed God, he has not loved God single-heartedly. What the person should do in the midst of new problems is to raise his Giving to God and have 30,000 for himself and the God of heaven will multiply this a hundredfold. So, what will that give? - Let me even just take tenfold.

70%   70,000   300,000

60%   ~~60,000~~   40,000

He has 300,000 now to live in the abundance of God. But he will first of all be tested. He will first of all be tested so that he's not playing games with God. He has gone up and now he is in the abundance of wealth. He is a king - wealth, wealth, wealth, wealth, wealth. But, if he sinks... So he has now risen to wealth, to spiritual knowledge, spiritual desire, and spiritual hunger. So his spiritual content will rise to this level. He now has more than enough for his needs and more to give to that God. It is a choice. And when a leader chooses to sink, he has committed the greatest sin for ever because he sinks with the people! He blocks the people since the destiny of the people is tied to the destiny of the leader before God. The destiny of the people is tied to the destiny of the leader before God

I've just taken one area to illustrate what I'm saying. The question is, "Who will solve my problems—God or me?" The question is, "Who will handle my new problems?"

"Who will handle my new responsibilities?"

It's a question as to whether a man believes that God is and that He's the Rewarder of those who diligently seek Him. And brethren, I'm saying it because I don't know one person who went back on what he gave to God and remained the same. And money really tells you who a man's god is. More than anything else, it tests the finest fibres in a man.

TIME SPENT ALONE WITH GOD IS WHAT MAKES A LEADER

How leadership is maintained – Time spent with God is indispensable for leadership

Tuesday, 25th October, 2005.

I don't know whether you go on retreats. I consider leaders who do not go on retreats one weekend a month sick— sick with the absence of God's presence because it is at retreats that a man gets saturated with God so that even just his presence, his person, his words, his touch might impart God to the others. I strongly recommend one weekend retreat a month, if not, you have chosen to be superficial. Maybe you can't go at weekends. If you can go in the middle of the week, do so. Two, three days every month, every month, every month will make you a normal believer, a normal believer. Reading some books lightly in passing will not help you. It would only have added to your deception. But on your knees before God, with time for God to deal with you, things will happen that will change you.

How much time is left? - Very little. Look at the world in the grip of the birth pangs that will precede the return of the Lord. If you are not troubled about how you would appear before Christ not long from now, then "Ashia[1]."

For those of you who have just believed, I encourage you with all my heart to read and read and read and read and read. During the twelve months of the year 1967, I read fifty Christian books. It gave me a solid foundation. In 1986, I spent twenty-six weekends on retreats. Their marks (the marks of those weekends) on my life cannot be counted. When I travelled with a brother, he asked me. "What happened?" At some point, others could not lay hold on me anymore. I told him, "Twenty-six retreats in 1986; it gave me so many jumps ahead of others."

The foundation of leadership is a life lost in God—enormous time spent in God's presence alone - because without this impartation of God, a man does not have what to give others; for leadership is a call to give God to others. You cannot have what you have not received. Just look at a man's development in being alone with God, then you know the person. If you are flirting before men going forward and backward in the guise of leadership, you are doing the Church of God great harm! If you are spending a lot of time with men and too little time with God, you are an enemy of those people because you don't have God to give them! If you have ideas, they are ideas without God. And it is great wickedness, great wickedness, great wickedness to give people ideas that are not impregnated with God. They will not change them. They will not transform them. They will not trouble them. You are a clown. You are an entertainer. <u>Leadership is a call to specialise in</u>

<u>God</u>. It is a call to specialise in God. <u>It is a call to major in God</u>; to major in God indeed. It is to make God your sole pursuit. Alone with God! Alone with God! Alone with God! Alone with God! Alone with God! Always seeking to withdraw and be alone with God, to plan a day for being alone with God so that God may give Himself to you!

I want to warn those who are not taking time, enough time, to specialise in God but who spend countless hours with men. I warn them in God's Name that they are doing harm to God, they are doing harm to God's cause and they are destroying those people. Leadership is a call to major in God, to concentrate on God, to possess God so that the person has God in abundance, so that his thoughts are saturated with God, his tastes are saturated with God, his desires are saturated with God, his motives are saturated with God, his attitude is saturated with God, his values are saturated with God, his tastes are saturated with God, his heart's disposition saturated with God, his words saturated with God, his possessions and his attitude to things saturated with God. There's a world of difference between superficial touches and saturation. For those of you who intend to be leaders someday, make God your unique pursuit. Make God your unique pursuit. Begin to seek Him ardently. Decide that you will spend ten thousand hours with God alone within a certain number of years, with nobody there, because the impartation of God takes place in the silence of a man and his God. Alone with God, alone with God, alone with God, alone with God, alone with God, alone with God - reading your Bible and weeping that you are not like what the Bible says and asking God to make you like what the Bible says, reading Christian Literature and crying out to God that what is written there will be written in your life by the Holy Spirit.

Of course, you can also choose to be superficial. God will force no one. But not long from now, at the Judgment Seat of Christ, you will have eternity to bemoan your lack of God-content. If you think that it is in one or two hours a day spent with God that you will come into the depths of God, then your self-deception is mighty beyond telling. The only way a shepherd can prove that he loves the flock is to spend so much time with God, so much time with God that he brings the abundance of God to the flock. The only way a shepherd can show that he loves the flock is to be so married to God, is to so penetrate the depths of God that even if he spends a few minutes with the flock, the flock has quantity food instead of spending hours clowning or giving them food without the depths of God. You have to choose whether to spend seven hours with God and one hour with the flock during which you really meet the needs of the flock or one hour with God and seven hours of dancing around without one transforming touch on the flock. The Scriptures can be quoted, "It is written," by a man who knows those words. It could also be quoted by a man who is pregnant with those words. The difference is enormous beyond telling.

Leadership, better said in French, is a call to "sonder les profondeurs de Dieu" – to pursue the depths of God because the leader asks, "What am I taking to these people?" – not entertaining stories, not beautiful phrases. Leadership is a call to bring God to the people. If you don't bring God to the people, you have ruined them, you have deceived them, you have betrayed them because the building of men is the impartation of divine imprints to them so that they can see and say, "Look at the marks of the Cross. Look at the marks of the Cross. Look at the marks of the Cross. Look at the spite of the world. Look at the despising of its vainglory. Look at the contentment in God" because the leader is not preoccupied with what he will tell the people. It is what he will give the people that matters to him. It is what his words will contain. It is what his words will impart. It is the transforming power, it is the troubling power, it is the stirring power, and it is the igniting power of his words that are decisive.

Have you asked yourself, "How much of God do I have? What is my God-content? How much of God flows through me?" Have you sought to know how deep you are? The secret of power or success in a man's ministry is that time that he spends before God alone so that God is imparted to him, so that he goes away with the abundance of God for himself and the abundance of God for others and so that he can give himself to tens, hundreds, thousands for long periods without exhaustion. The one who loves the flock specialises in God. The one who hates the flock specialises in men. In fact, you would be wise if you made God your only pursuit. You would be wise if you made God your only Treasure. But treasure has to be sought, pursued, found and owned. If God is not given to the people, then the people are betrayed. So the leader is called to have God at all cost. The leader is called to have God at all costs. The leader is called to have God in over-flowing abundance. That is his calling. How about you, is that your calling? Is that your calling? If it is not, I charge you, in the name of the living God to repent.

We have a lot of Campaigns going on. If people who have not soaked themselves in God stand before people to proclaim eternal realities, they would do great harm because human words can produce decisions. However, they will not produce conversions. The words that are spirit and life come from the impartation of spirit and life in the closet with God alone. This is what it ought to be. That's what it must be, if a man does not want to find himself opposing God. Now, I want to charge you before the living God to never, never, never, never mount the pulpit in the name of the living God without being saturated with God. This is basic honesty. You cannot build for eternity with superficiality. You can only build for eternity along with God.

I have been meditating since last week on the first three verses of John chapter 21. While in a backslidden condition, Peter says. "I'm going fishing." Seven other disciples too say, "We are going with you" He was followed. But he didn't have God. To have a large following without God is a crime against heaven! The whole of that night they caught nothing.

What are the results of your life? What are your imprints on others? What do you have of God in abundance? Where are you filled with the fullness of God? When did you give God large chunks of time for Him to fill you with the fullness of God?

Look at your disciples. Where are the marks of Christ on them? Look at those who are most intimately related to you. Are they crucified men and women? Are they consecrated men and women? Are they burdened for the glory of God? Are they pursuers of God? If not, you are a problem. Your God-content is shallow! Go and seek God until you are possessed by that which changes men, until you are filled with that which transforms men. There are no shortcuts in these things and there are no alternatives for anyone who is honest.

THE LEADER IS PRODUCED YEARS BEFORE HE BECOMES A LEADER

Being, Doing, Having

The leader is not produced in public; the example of the Lord Jesus Christ

Tuesday, 14th February, 2006.

We already had two lessons on the marks of a leader. In the first lesson we saw that a person leads by being ahead of the people he leads. We said that the leader is ahead! The leader is ahead! The leader is ahead! If you are at the same level with people, you cannot lead them. You lead them by being ahead! By being ahead! By being ahead! They look at the person and he's ahead, he's ahead, he's ahead, he's ahead, he's ahead so those who are led follow, those who are led follow. So we said then that the leader leads by might, by deeds of might. That was the first lesson.

The second lesson: we said that in leadership the one who is a leader has to pay the same price that he paid to become a leader and a greater price in order to maintain his leadership. He must pay the same price that he paid to become a leader in order to maintain leadership. If he stops paying the price, he stops being a leader. For a man to continue to be a leader, the minimum is that he pays the price that he was paying before he became a leader. Normally, he should pay a greater price. If he was praying for two hours before he became a leader, he must pray a minimum of two hours. In fact, to be candid, brethren, he must pay a greater price. The price that was paid before a man became a leader must be exceeded for him to maintain leadership. If I prayed two hours, to maintain myself spiritually in the right condition, to maintain my wife in the right condition, to maintain our children in the right condition, then when I become a leader and continue to pray for two hours, I will fail. Why? I now have the people, I still have myself, and I still have my family. Therefore, I must now pray more in order to carry the people that I am leading; because now, my wife is under greater pressure because of my leadership. I am under greater pressure because of my leadership and have the people that I am leading to carry in prayer. So if I don't increase my praying, I've spelt disaster for myself, for my wife, for our children and for the people I lead. My fasting life must increase. Whatever I did before I became a leader, I must do it now at a greater scale. Why? I am now the enemy's target. Yes, as a leader, I am now the enemy's target. The devil tells his agents, "Fight only with this man who is the leader." I am now the devil's target. My wife is now the devil's target. Our children are now the devil's target. And the people I lead are the devil's target. Therefore, I must intensify my fasting in order that all may go well. If my holiness could be described at levels, if I was at level 3 in holiness, O, because I have become a leader, I must push up the level of my holiness to at least Level 4.

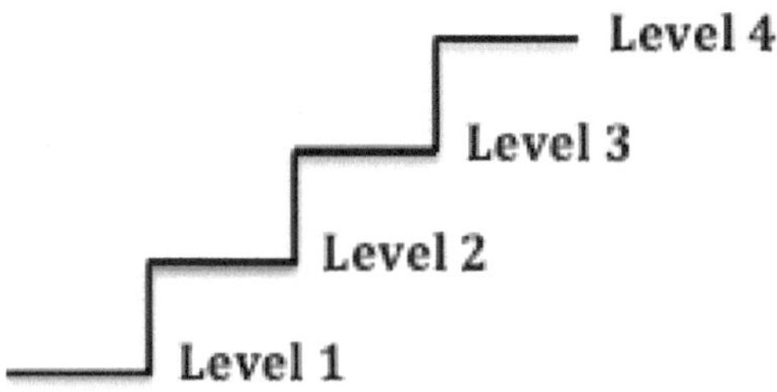

Why? If I'm not holier than I was before, I will crumble. There are sins that can be overlooked in the ranks and files of the army. There are sins that can be overlooked in the ordinary soldiers that cannot be tolerated in the generals! Look, brethren, the children of Israel were murmuring almost every day. The whole trip was a trip of murmuring. But when Moses sinned once, he was disqualified. There are sins that can be overlooked in the people led. If they are found in the leader, he will be destroyed, removed by God or put aside while he buffoons before men. A greater price must be paid. That was the second lesson.

Pray that these two lessons would find their place in the hearts— would find their place in the hearts of the current leaders and the future leaders.

We move to Lesson Three, In fact, Lesson Three ought to be Lesson One. For the leader, the determinant thing is what we call "the hidden years." The hidden years—long before he became the leader -- that is when the leader is really produced. The leader is not produced in public, the leader is not produced when he becomes a leader! The leader is produced years before he is ever considered for leadership. His training takes place over very many years in the ordinary business of life. It is how he performs in the ordinary business of life that will move him to become a leader or put him aside completely, because the leader is first of all what he is, his being! The leader is first of all, his being. It is secondly his doing, and it may be his possessing.

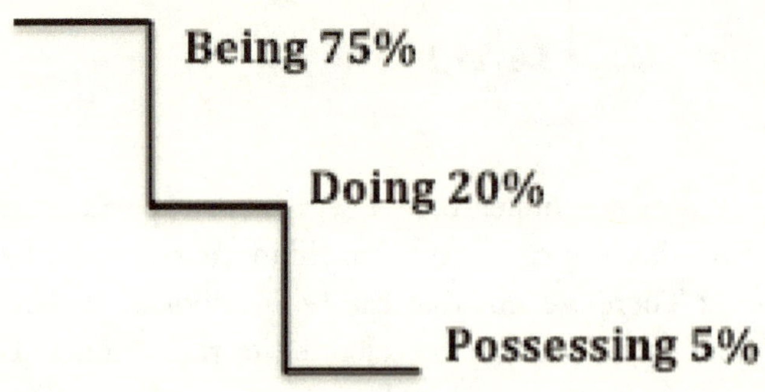

Godly Leadership

For me, his Being – is 75%, his Doing – is 20% of what it takes to be a leader, and his Possessing contributes 5% of his credentials for leadership. Listen, brethren, that's what it is in the Lord. In the world, it is different. In the world, it is your Possessing – 75%, and your Being 5%.

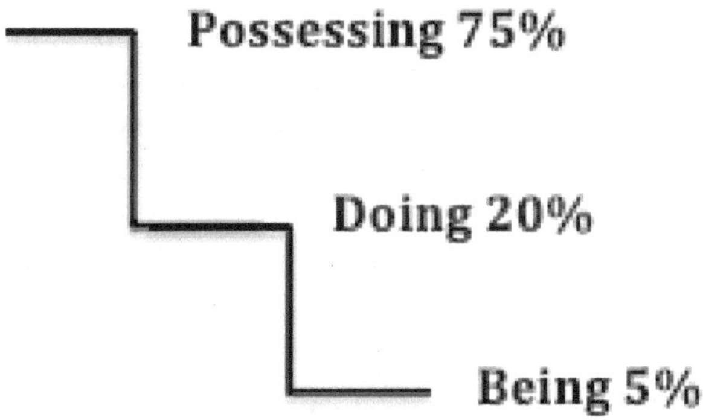

Worldly Leadership

A brother told me that somebody was chased out of his village for outrageous conduct. Yes, he was banished from the village for being corrupt in every way. He became a "fey man" (swindler) and made fortune beyond measure. He came back and tarred all the streets in the village. The same people who had exiled him met and gave him the highest title in the village. Nothing had changed. However, he had increased his possessions enormously through crookery, through evil, and had tarred the streets. His being had not changed, yet they gave him the highest title in the village. That's worldly leadership.

O, Jesus Christ is the Supreme Leader! The Supreme Leader! He had no place to lay His head. He possessed nothing. Whatever He used was borrowed. O, but He was mighty in His Being! Mighty in His Being! His whole Being was God incarnate! His character was the very Being of God and His Doings were powerful. However His Doings were only secondary. In the Lord Jesus Christ, what matters is what the man is. That's determinant, that's determinant, that's determinant. What he does is secondary. What he possesses is of no consequence. Brethren, with regards to a work of God, it is the character of the people involved that matters. The being is essentially the character – the inward purity, the inward dying to self, the taking up of the Cross, the suffering day by day, the love towards God, the joy in God's presence, the peace that comes from God, the patience with regards to God, the kindness towards man, the goodness towards man, the faithfulness to God and to man, the gentleness to man and the self-control in all things - that is the man. That is the man. The being is the fruit of the Spirit.

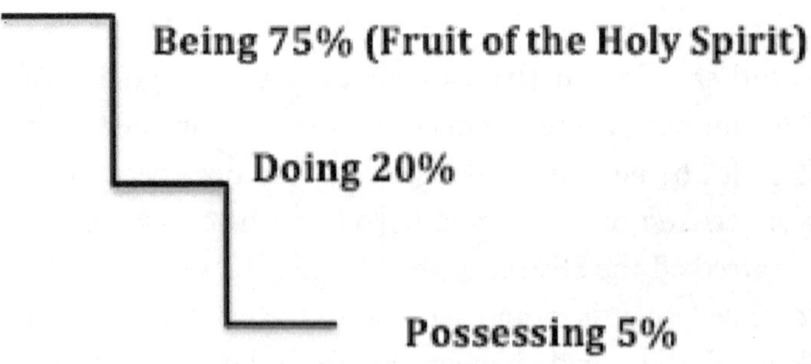

The Doing - the aspect of mighty deeds is a matter of power —the power of spiritual gifts. The doing is the release of spiritual gifts and the flow of consecrated talents. That's what helps the doing. A believer produces results as the overflow of spiritual gifts and as the overflow of consecrated talents. Therefore, the one who does not have many gifts and many talents doesn't suffer from a heavy disadvantage because the 75% of his being remains intact (at the top). I beg you to see it. In the light of eternal reward, it is "Well done, good and faithful servant." This is essentially character isn't it? Good – the fruit of the Spirit – goodness, faithfulness that is also the fruit of the Spirit.

Because the leader is essentially his being and much less of his doing, the making of the spiritual leader takes place long before he comes to the open. Brethren, allow me to start with the example of our Supreme Lord,

> *"O Lord Jesus, who is worthy to talk about*
> *You? Who is worthy to talk about You?*
> *I'm worthless! Worthless! Worthless!*
> *Lord, we plead, O God, that Your holi-*
> *ness might clothe us and cover us as we*
> *dare to speak about You, for You are*
> *beyond human speech, beyond human*
> *discussion, beyond human analysis. O*
> *God, even the dust upon Thy feet arrests*
> *us totally. Help us to learn from You, in*
> *Jesus" Name. Amen."*

The Lord Jesus Christ came to seek and to save that which was lost. He was programmed to spend thirty-three-and-a-half years on earth. He was programmed from eternity to spend thirty-three-and-a-half years on earth. What did He do? How did He divide this time? Thirty years in preparation, three-and-a-half years in public action. Preparation was in private action. Thirty years in preparing the being and three-and-a-half years into doing the deeds. Brethren, I realised this and I was shocked. He spent 30 years in preparing the Minister and three-and-a-half years in being the Minister. Pray that this will be grasped by all of us.

In Hebrews 2:10 the Bible says,

> *In bringing many sons to glory, it was fitting that God, for Whom*
> *and through whom everything exists, should make the Author of*
> *their salvation perfect through suffering.*

Jesus was made perfect through suffering before He took on leadership, before He came to the limelight.

In Hebrews 5:7-9,

> *During the days of Jesus' life on earth, he offered up prayers and petitions with loud cries and tears to the One who could save him from death, and he was heard because of his reverent submission. Although he was a Son, he learned obedience from what he suffered and once made perfect, he became the source of eternal salvation for all who obey him.*

− It says, although He was the Son of God, He learned obedience through what He suffered. He learned obedience through what He suffered. Jesus had to learn obedience through the things He suffered. So for thirty years He was preparing behind the scene − for thirty years! Brethren, He was preparing for a public Ministry that would last only three-and-a-half years. Jesus had four brothers and at least two sisters. His brothers were unbelievers and He lived in that home for thirty years, being trained through difficult circumstances, being trained through difficult circumstances right in His family − the persecution of His family. He was without sin in spite of all the mockery for bringing, (as if it were,) what we could call strange standards. For thirty years He lived as an ordinary human being. And the training was going on. And the testing was going on at home. He became a businessman and had to provide for the family. It seems as if Joseph had died early because he disappeared from the Scriptures. And Jesus was the firstborn; so He had to provide for the family. He didn't sit there and say. "O Son of God; Son of God." He worked hard! He worked hard! He worked hard! He worked hard and He learnt carpentry! He learnt carpentry! He learnt carpentry! He learnt carpentry! He did not bring carpentry from heaven! He did not bring carpentry skills from heaven! He learnt carpentry on earth! We insist that He learnt carpentry on earth. He got through the discipline of going to a professional school which might have been just that one carpenter took Him and He learnt from that man. He learnt from that man and learnt from that man and learnt from that man, from the simple things and on and on until He mastered the art of carpentry. We rebuke the lazy! We rebuke the lazy! We rebuke the lazy! Sick and lazy! Sick and lazy! Sick and lazy! Sick and lazy! They have no place in the Church because they have no resemblance to the Master! O, the Lord Jesus Christ went and learnt carpentry. The Lord Jesus Christ went and learnt carpentry. He learnt carpentry and He mastered carpentry. And He mastered carpentry: And there was a day when He started His own business. He had to learn the art of buying wood, buying nails and buying everything and making furniture that was sold. And He sold and made profit for Himself and for His family. O, He learnt, He learnt, He learnt, He learnt. He learnt the suffering through carpentry, the suffering through business. He learnt through being honest among dishonest people. He learnt to be true to God in business. O Jesus was a businessman! Jesus was a businessman! O Jesus was a businessman! Jesus was a businessman! And in all those years, not once did He sin; not once was He corrupt; not once did He fail in delivering the goods. When they mocked Him they said, "Is this not the carpenter?" They didn't say, "Is this not the carpenter who did not deliver the goods I asked Him to make? Who did not deliver the goods that I paid for?" They didn't ask, "Is this not the carpenter who delivered the goods two weeks after He promised?" - Character! Character! Character! Character at home and character at the workplace! Character at home and character at the workplace! And it is in these two places that a person trains for leadership – the home, the workplace; the home, the workplace; the home, the workplace. The one who fails at home has failed. The one who fails at his work place has failed.

Brethren, I am just overwhelmed by the errors that we have made. We have appointed people to leadership who did not pass the test of the home, who have not passed the test about the place of work. And we have sent these people to the mission field. They have not known how to earn money, manage it, save some and provide all their needs. And we have sent them to go and lead people – How will they go about it? On what basis will they advise a married man with his wife and children?

A boy of perhaps twenty-two, twenty-three, twenty-five or even thirty, doesn't know what marriage is about. He takes the girl that we paid the bride price for him to marry. He has never earned money. He doesn't know the agony of earning money. He starts by spending the money that is the fruit of the sweat of others. What model will he be? What leadership can he provide? That is not the Saviour's model.

It's said of the Lord Jesus Christ, Hebrews 2:17-18,

> *For this reason He had to be made like His brothers in every way, in order that He might become a merciful and faithful High Priest in service to God, and that He might make atonement for the sins of the people. Because He Himself suffered when He was tempted, He is able to help those who are being tempted.*

He was tempted, He made progress, He learnt at home to be holy regardless of what the environment was. He was holy in His profession regardless of what the other carpenters were doing. He was holy, holy, tempted, tempted, tempted, tempted, but without sin. He did not yield, He did not yield,

He did not yield, He did not yield, He did not yield to the temptation to make quick money. He did not say, "Father, let someone come and pay 500,000 francs for this thing that sells for 5000 francs." He did not expect God to violate the laws of business and provide.

There are some people who are expecting that they would wake up someday and gain possession of big shops filled with things, and they working there. They are expecting a miracle that will just double their sales, triple their sales, increase it a hundredfold. They are waiting to wake up to a title deed for a thousand square metres and a three-storey building. This is just corruption, brother! It is wicked dreams! Wicked dreams!

Jesus did not appeal for miraculous provision in His business. He practised the law of being good and faithful. At home, He was good and faithful at work, He was good and faithful! Good, faithful, good and faithful, good and faithful, good and faithful, good and faithful, good and faithful, good and faithful, good and faith-ful, good and faithful! Listen, brethren; He was good and faithful at home, without sin at home. He was good and faithful at work. At home, He got the Father's approval that He was without sin, that He was good and that He was faith-ful. At home, He obtained the Father's approval that He was without sin, He was good and He was faithful. And at His job, He obtained the Father's approval that He was without sin, that He was good and He was faithful. This went on for very many years, for very many years: for thirty years, for thirty years, for thirty years, thirty years.

He was not in debt. He was not in debt. He was not in debt because debt greatly undermines integrity! The debtor is a man without integrity, a sick man who wants to have what he doesn't have money for. A debtor is corrupt and rotten inside, corrupt and rotten, corrupt and rotten. He wants to have what he doesn't have money for. It can only be a step outside God's will that will only bring him heartache and heartache and tragedy, because when God gives a project, He provides the funds. If there are no funds, the project is not from God or it's not in God's timing. Jesus was not in debt.

I want to insist that Jesus made profit. He provided for His mother. He provided for His brothers and sisters. The Bible says, "He who does not provide for his household is worse than an infidel and has denied the faith."

1Timothy 5:8,

> *If anyone does not provide for his relatives, and especially for his immediate family, he has denied the faith and is worse than an unbeliever.*

Jesus was faithful in providing for His family. He employed His hands and His head to provide for His family. He used His hands and His head to earn money to meet the needs of his family. Instead of working, you want to beg and beg and beg. God can never make you a leader. If men make you a leader, God will pull you down because you have not passed the test. For thirty-three years, Jesus had been preparing, brethren! At the age of twelve, at the temple, He baffled the religious leaders of the day. They were baffled by His knowledge.

He could have started His Ministry then but it would have ended in failure because He had not learnt yet. From twelve to thirty He entered the school of character formation—how to live honestly, how to live in integrity, how to be faithful at home and at work, how to earn one's money honestly, how to spend that which was earned, how not to spend what one doesn't have. The family of Jesus was poor. When He was eight days old and taken to the temple to be presented, his parents did not present the lamb that was expected. They brought the gift that was prescribed for the poor.

> *If she cannot afford a lamb, she is to bring two doves or two young pigeons, one for a burnt offering and the other for a sin offering. In this way the priest will make atonement for her, and she will be clean* (Leviticus 12:8).

That is what the poor presented. Those who were well off presented a lamb. Jesus did not say, "Let Me look for a rich family to live with." Jesus did not look for more comfortable quarters He identified Himself with His family as their servant; He identified Himself with His family in their poverty and accelerated the putting on of perfect character, holy character. Until thirty, He was unknown for anything extraordinary. But He put on the being, the being, the being, the being and the doing of ordinary things extraordinarily; faithful in small matters, faithful in little things, faithful in little things, faithful in little things. After thirty years, He was ready to provide leadership. His innocence as a child had been transformed into holiness through the events and the circumstances of His life.

We must look at the matter of preparing people in private. They are prepared in private as they interact with ordinary things, and they mature there. Leadership is not for babies. They may be zealous, they may have ideals but it is untried idealism, and because that kind of idealism can crack and the idealist becomes a criminal, it has to be tempered in the school of life without which a man is not fit for leadership.

About John the Baptist, Luke 1:80 states:

And the child grew and became strong in spirit; and he lived in the desert until he appeared publicly to Israel.

He grew in spirit. The human spirit of John grew. Growth in the spirit - the tragedy of our generation is that we send people to be trained only in the mind. There is no training of the emotions, there is no training of the will, and of course, there is no training of the spirit, there is no training of the conscience, there is no training of the intuition and communion.

Of Jesus Christ it was said (Luke 2:40),

And the Child grew and became strong; he was filled with wisdom, and the grace of God was upon Him

— as a child.

I hope that's what you people are training the children to become. This is before He became a youth. This is the child Jesus between nought and twelve years. And the child grew and became strong; he was filled with wisdom and the grace of God was upon Him." Then at the age of twelve, He went to the temple. He was a youth. That's the behind-the-scenes preparation of Jesus!

PATHWAYS TO SPIRITUAL LEADERSHIP

The hidden years

The example of the parents of John the Baptist

Tuesday, 21st February, 2006

What lies behind the man or the woman who makes impact for God? The first thing in the making of a spiritual leader is their parents! Their parents! Their parents! Their parents! Their parents! Their parents! We looked at the model of Jesus last time. This time we'll look at the model of His forerunner.

In Luke 1:5 we read,

In the time of Herod king of Judea there was a priest named Zechariah, who belonged to the priestly division of Abijah; his wife Elizabeth was also a descendant of Aaron.

Ha! Ha! Ha! Listen, each person is influenced a great deal by what his roots are! Each person is determined by his roots. A sister did something I found very strange. When I was trying to fume, she told me, "Ça vient de loin, de ma grand-mere. (It comes way back, from my grandmother.)" And I was disarmed. "Ça vient de loin." Sometimes you see children who don't resemble their parents rather they resemble their grandparents.

This is one of the most beautiful stories in the whole Bible, because, generally when you see a great man, you find his wife doing some funny things. When you see a great woman you find her husband doing some strange things. But listen, Zechariah was a man of great spiritual weight. His wife Elizabeth was a woman of the glory. She is one of the women whom we are going to write a book on - one of the women of the glory. The priestly division of Abijah, Abijah the prophet - so John came from a prophetic line. He came from a prophetic line. His wife was of Aaron's lineage.

O brethren, you may feel sorry as you look at your background but you cannot run away from this fact, that the background is crucially important. In what book did we write about Jonathan Edwards and Mark Jules? A woman gets pregnant and gives birth, "Peng - Hmmm[1]" - a criminal comes out. Another time, another pregnancy, "Eh![3]" - a criminal comes out. A third time, "Pai! Pai! Pai! Pai![4]" a criminal comes out. I'm going to say something which I said in Indonesia and one of the people in the conference, an American woman, called me and told me, "You deserve to be shot. What you have said is too true." I had said that if a boy wants to get married, he should not look at the girl. He should look at her parents, - her father and her mother. And if he has access to her grandparents, he should look at them - grandfather and grandmother. This beauty you see now will soon not be there;

thereafter, you will live with her grandparents or her mother, her father, all your life. If I were a girl, if a boy came to me, I would not look at him. I would look at his parents and grandparents, if I have access to them; because when the flattering words that say, "O you are the most beautiful one" will be gone, you'll be married to his father and his grandfather.

If his father was a thief, you will live with the thief; if he was godless, you will live with a godless man; if he was a squanderer of money, the son will exaggerate it; if he never pursued God, if he never pursued God, the son will go in that direction. If he walked with God and backslid, the son will follow suite. If he was radical for God ... Listen, if he was a Catholic and radically committed, it's good. If he was a Presbyterian and radically committed, it's good. I want to go further, if he was a Moslem and radically committed, it's good, because the radically committed in spiritual matters, when they confront the truth, will also pursue it radically. Those who are light-hearted about the truth, even if they are Pentecostals, will always be light-hearted. The one who, as an idol-worshipper tilts towards the spiritual seeing it as central and determinant, when he meets the Lord Jesus Christ, will have the spiritual as central and determinant. You can see how Paul was violently opposed to the Lord Jesus after he was converted. O! He was on fire, burning, and was committed to Jesus Christ. The background, the background, the background, the background!

My father shook the village. My father shook the village. I only saw the foundation of the Church in the village. It was 18 metres by 12 metres. I measured it. Only the foundation is left. That's what he built. If I were not zealous, I would be the worst criminal. That my younger sister fasts is only a product of that. They sang,

> *"O Papa Solomon,*
> *Ou loye ni nge yaye yi*
> *O lin nga nje ni zangti*
> *Ou lo ye m nge ya ye yi."*
> *"O Papa Solomon[2],*
> *O where are you taking us to?*
> *Don't you know that we are hungry?"*

He used to preach long sermons. So while he was preaching one day, the people started to sing and say, "O don't you know that we are hungry?" So, warn me to stop, before the congregation starts singing. You should warn me to jump out before they start singing. When that brother said here the other day that the programme says, "Five o'clock," I got it as a warning.

But listen; God has given you the opportunity to be the starting point of a radical generation madly in love with Jesus Christ, madly committed to Him so that what you did not have in your background, your great-grandchildren would have. But look, brethren, you are compromising it! You are compromising it! You are compromising it! You are divided at heart! You are divided at heart! You are backslidden. What a sad thing! You've gone back to sin, you are telling your progeny that they too shall go back to sin. You've gone back to loving the world! You have gone back to debts to curse your progeny! How terrible! How terrible! How terrible! How terrible! How terrible! How terrible! – A man who saw light and went back on it, a man who had dealings with God on an issue and then abandoned the dealings with God and went back to his vomit. The starting point, the starting point, the starting point!

As I said, my brother's daughter in the United States, who is 28, has bought an apartment of 1.3 million dollars – the blessings of my father. Even his only child who is in the country, was the only black person in the World Women's Tennis Championship. From a righteous man there will flow blessings in all domains. His first son, was at the World Scrabble Championship in November. I've shared with you how my father turned down a salary of 18 pence from the administration to accept one penny from the Missionaries as salary.

Brother, it will follow you— your decisions, your deeds. The question is: What are you providing − solid character or diffuse compromise? Are you true to what God first showed you? Are you true to your first vows to God? But remember, you are the starting point, you are the starting point regardless of what your parents were; but what type of starting point - an alloy or pure metal, rock or sand?

Listen brethren, my mother was a believer too, but she loved the world. She contributed enormously to my father's ministry. She was at the base. She was a practical woman who made "akra" (local fritters). Sometimes she baked bread, did farming and other things. She provided, she provided. She was a disciplinarian. She never said, "Wait for Papa to come." If you needed to be flogged, she just flogged you. However, she loved the world. That's why I've talked very little about her. When she was about 60 − these are just approximations − I brought her slides. I said, "Mama, here you are." She said, "Eh, bring my glasses quickly, let me see what dress I was wearing." At 60, she wanted to see what dress she was wearing. She earned money. In fact, she was three times richer than my father because my father was paid 10,000 francs cfa a month at the height of his pastoral ministry. There was good food. She had refined tastes since she came from the palace in Besi. You know in the palace there is luxury and finesse. That has come through very strongly. I've told you how many pairs of shoes my brother had. In Mutengene alone, I counted 57 pairs, some of ostrich skin from Australia.

He had suits of 450,000 francs cfa each. When he came for Parliament, he sometimes came with four suitcases of clothes. He told me, "You can dress like a catechist. I'm a businessman and before one talks business with you, he looks at your car and at your dressing. Emmanuel Fomum who is in Mbale, was in the School of Youth and Sports. In his first year, he had a monthly allowance of 97,000 old francs. I had paid all his fees for admission into the school. When he came, I asked him to bring me 50,000 francs each month so that I save it for him. I only saw him after four months. His room was carpeted. He had a fridge in it. He bought shoes for 25,000 francs. That's my mother's trait in evidence. In America, you can pay money so that your car number plate bears your name. My brother's son, the one who went for the Scrabble Championship had his car number plate of his name. There's no time to talk about it. So two tendencies run in the family —radical commitment to Christ and radical love of the world.

Brother, when you choose your wife, it's a frightful thing you might have done. You may desire that only your traits would be imparted to your offspring, but it's not possible. When you accept a man, you have done a far-reaching thing. You may desire only your strengths to be seen but you will see that man in your children and grandchildren. In particular, you will see the strengths or the corruptions of character. You will see the strengths of character or the crumbling of character. Therefore when you are thinking about this new foundation, ask: Is your wife as consecrated as you? Is she as consecrated as you? Is she as sold out to God as you or is she a "Lot's wife?" Is she mad about your vision, sold to it, paying the supreme price for it; or while you are flying she is crawling, when you are flying she is walking? Is she a woman of equivalent consecration? Is he a man of equivalent consecration?

But in the case of John the Baptist, it says "BOTH OF THEM! BOTH OF THEM!" Hallelujah! "BOTH OF THEM!" (Luke 1: 6a) Brethren, I am a reader of biographies – spiritual biographies and secular biographies – because I have been a student of the secret of powerful leadership for long. It is very rare that you find what is said here. "Both of them were upright in the sight of God." Hallelujah! "Upright in the sight of God; upright" – both, father, mother, Zechariah and Elizabeth. Both of them were upright. Both had great backgrounds rooted in spirituality, and now at the personal level, both of them were upright in the sight of God. Both of them! Both of them! Both of them! Both of them! Both of them! Upright! Upright! Upright! Upright! Upright! Upright! Upright! Upright! Upright! Upright! Upright! Upright! There was no moral failure. There was no moral decadence in the sight of God. God said about both of them, "Upright! Upright! Upright! Upright! Upright! Upright! Upright! Upright!" Hallelujah! "In the sight of God." They were not only upright. It was not just stupendous character! It was not just stupendous character! But they observed all the Lord's commandments and regulations blamelessly. Their character and their deeds got God's highest approval. "Upright in the sight of God, observing ALL the Lord's commandments, ALL the Lord's commandments." I want you to take "ALL" into consideration Both, both were upright and both observed the Lord's commandments. There is no room to disobey God in one thing. "ALL the Lord's commandments! ALL the Lord's commandments! ALL the Lord's commandments!" They were not upright in some things and not in others. "ALL the Lord's commandments! ALL the Lord's commandments"!

May the Holy Spirit convict you! May the Holy Spirit convict you! May the Holy Spirit trouble you! You violator of God's law! You violator of God's law! You violator of God's law! You violator of God's law! You violator of God's law! May the Holy Spirit trouble you! May the Holy Spirit trouble you! May God give you no peace! May God war against you now! May God war against you now and convict you and trouble you and trouble you and war against your seared conscience, and war against your seared conscience and war against your disobediences in the secrecy of your heart.

Brethren, I am working out every detail of obedience to God in my heart in everything in my life along this fast. I had a bed in my inner office. The Lord asked me to dismantle it. I had earlier dismantled it then I brought it back. I've dismantled it forever. For a laxative, "bitter-kola" helped me to relieve myself and I kept going to the toilet throughout the fast. Even on the twenty-third day, I went to the toilet; henceforth every fast has been ended with ease. Before, I used to sit on that first day as I went to stool. "Chei! Chei! Chei[3]!" It will be paining; try to sit on the other corner, I felt excruciating pain as if my anus would tear or give way. Some of you know what I am saying. But with the "bitter-kola," the faeces kept coming out slowly all through. I have stopped eating it. (Dr. Ngufor had to go digging in there in order to get the faeces out. In fact, as one thought about the end of the fast, that was what one dreaded.) But I've stopped it because the Lord told me, "I have no problem, but the Devil will resist you with it." So there will never be "bitter-kola" again during the fast so that the Devil does not resist me.

They say about Zechariah and Elizabeth, "observing all the Lord's commandments and regulations" not only the commandments but the regulations. Not only the commandments but the regulations! One thing which I would obey from now on without negotiation: the Lord commanded me to go to the Department every day I am in the city for two hours unfailingly because of World Conquest Science, and not to counsel anybody, not to discuss anything about the Lord in my office at all, at all, at all, but to give these two hours exclusively to Science. Brethren, "all the commandments" are the Logos of God while "the regulations" are a special Rhema of God to you. "All the Lord's commandments and all the Lord's regulations."

Listen brethren, it's for your good. It's for my good. Two years ago, the Lord told me, "Don't take *Plenyl*[4] during your fasts, take *Supradyne*[5]." Now *Supradyne* to me is the worst drug. You drop it in water and it becomes a terrible thing. Last year, a new *Supradyne* was made that tastes better. In addition, it has some vitamins that will help the body of a man who is over 50; it is "Vital 50+." This was made for me. These are the encouragements of God in the pathway of obedience. What am I saying? I am talking of a very personal God who comes to be involved in the minutest details. I was wondering what would happen to me to enable me stool with ease. Now I found out that Magnesium functions as a laxative. So the faeces comes out easily. God had said, "No more bitter-kola." But I don't have problem with passing out faeces. I've gone to toilet every day in the last three days. It is settled. There is a living God – The Lord's commandments; the Lord's regulations!

It's wonderful. Brethren – upright, obedient and blameless – husband and wife, husband and wife, what a couple! What a couple! They had no children. Elizabeth was barren. They were advanced in years—very many years of uprightness, of uprightness, of uprightness in the sight of God; very many years of observing all the Lord's commandments; very many years of observing all the Lord's regulations, Hallelujah!

I want to say the next thing about John the Baptist's parents. Zechariah and Elizabeth were descendants of Aaron. Aaron was a priest. Zechariah pursued faithfulness; he did not pursue greatness. He pursued faithfulness. He did routine things in an extraordinary way. He did not go seeking for lions to kill. He just carried out the routine things in an extraordinary way - faithful, faithful, faithful, faithful, faithful, faithful, every year - faithful, faithful, faithful; every month - faithful, faithful, faithful, faithful; every day - faithful, faithful; every hour - faithful, faithful; every minute - faithful, faithful, faithful - with the right heart and faithfulness in duty, in doing what was assigned to him. He went to the temple of the Lord by lot to burn the incense.

Luke 1:10,

> *And when the time for the burning of incense came, all the assem-*
> *bled worshippers were praying outside.*

Listen! "All the assembled worshippers were praying outside!" - ALL! ALL! ALL! ALL! ALL the assembled worshippers! ALL the assembled worshippers! ALL! ALL! ALL! ALL! ALL! ALL were outside. Doing what? – praying, praying, praying, praying, praying, praying, praying, praying, praying, praying, praying; all outside, all outside; praying, praying, praying, praying; all, all, all, all; praying, praying, praying. One man was inside, all the others were praying. One man was at the place of burning incense while all the others were at the place of prayer.

I've seen great things happen in Bujumbura, in Burundi, because immediately I go to the stage, since the stage is built over the prayer room that is below, the intercessors just move there. I noticed a sister, she started going there immediately I went on stage. From both sides, brethren went in there. While I was preaching, they were blasting heaven! While I was preaching, they were blasting heaven. No wonder, people were weeping on the ground over their sins. People came to the Lord weeping and weeping. So many miracles happened that those who were healed came out and they had to drag us down from the stage lest we cause the stage to collapse. We brought back testimonies upon testimonies of miracles. A man on the pulpit, the rest or very many others blasting heaven and calling God's power upon him: While his word went out, the brethren brought down God's power upon the word. While the word of God was released, the power of God was brought down. So the word flowed in the power of the Holy Spirit! Yeah!

...When the time for the burning of incense came, all the assembled worshippers were praying outside, praying outside (Verse 10).

Praying outside, praying outside, praying outside, and praying outside

As they were praying, an angel of the Lord appeared to him. Hallelujah! Their prayers brought down an angel. Their prayers brought down an angel. Yes, you don't even have one person who prays for you. Do you hope angels will come? They will not! That's what it says, isn't it? "All the assembled worshippers were praying outside. Then! Then! Then an angel of the Lord appeared to him" - that's Zechariah (Verse 11a). While they were praying, an angel came. While they were praying, an angel came – Gabriel. While they were praying, an angel came.

You can now understand. When I came back from China. I said, "God said this." "God appeared to me. He laid His hands on me. "The Lord Jesus Christ appeared" and so on, because during those ten days, in our Ministry the whole world was praying for me, the Prayer Chains at Etoug-Ebe went on non-stop. I've had my clearest revelations during those times in

2001; and that's the only time I've seen the Lord Jesus Christ, He came into the room. In fact, He stood at the door and He showed me my "Separation from the Common" just as D. had typed it. He showed me and He said, "You are not living this out in fullness." Then He walked out in anger. That's the only time I saw the Lord Jesus Christ. God the Father has appeared to me four times. The last time He came in, He laid His hands on me. When He came, I was so overwhelmed, I knelt on the bed. I was not frightened. This was the first time I was not frightened. It was sweet and He laid His hands on me and said eighty-four things. The Lord laid His hand on my head and He said 84 things. He said twelve things, each one of them seven times. All the Brethren in our Ministry, were praying, it was their prayers that brought God down.

> *All the assembled worshippers were praying outside. Then an angel of the Lord appeared to him* (Verses 10b-11a).

God is brought down by prayer. God is brought down by prayer. Fasting shatters the Devil. Prayer brings God down.

Luke 3:21-22b says,

> *As He was praying, heaven was opened and the Holy Spirit descended on Him in bodily form like a dove.*

As He was praying, the Holy Spirit came down. Strong prayers bring such mighty descents of the Holy Spirit. That's the lacking element. If God is to descend, men must pray. If the power of the Holy Spirit is to descend, men must pray. If the power of the Holy Spirit is to descend on all, all must pray and keep on praying until He comes down. Incense was going up to God, and prayer was going up to God. There is the incense of a holy life rising up unceasingly to God. There is the incense of a holy life, the incense of a pure heart rising up unceasingly to God and then prayer to bring God down. During the Prayer Night, we saw that the fastest way out of poverty is not to receive but to give what you have. The fastest way out of poverty is not to receive but to give. Incense was going up. Prayer was going up. And then the angel came. What did he say?

Your prayer has been heard (Luke 1: 13b).

God did not answer immediately. "Your prayer has been heard." They prayed for many years. God heard but God took His time. Since they were holy, righteous people, their prayers went right to the Throne but God did not send the answer immediately. He didn't send them a son immediately. Why? Had he come immediately, had the son come immediately, he would have been ordinary. O, John was to be the forerunner of the Lord Jesus Christ! He was to be the forerunner of Jesus Christ! Therefore, his parents had to be childless for years, for long years, long years, long years so that John would come just before Jesus. Had he come earlier, he would have been ordinary. He was to go before Jesus! He was to go before Jesus! Therefore, he had to come just before Jesus — a six-month difference. It was of the utmost importance that this couple be barren for years! It was of the utmost importance that this couple be barren for years! It was of the utmost importance that this couple's prayers go as if God were not hearing so that the son born might be the son that he was meant to be!

Do you know the whole matter of the timing of God! The timing of God! The timing of God! Don't be like the brothers of Jesus Christ. He said,

My time has not yet come but your time is always here (John 7:6, RSV).

The timing of God! The timing of God! The timing of God! The timing of God! The timing of God! The timing of God! O people of God, people of God wake up, wake up, wake up, to the timing of God! The timing of God! The timing of God! The timing of God! The timing of God! The timing of God! The timing of God! Are you plugged into the timing of God? Are you plugged into the timing of God? Are you plugged into the timing of God? The timing of God! The timing of God! The timing of God! If God had answered maybe ten years before or twenty years before so that the couple should feel good, he would not have been what he was meant to be. It was crucial that Elizabeth bore the marks of a barren woman for years, that Elizabeth be a barren woman for years. It was important! It was important! It was important so that things might synchronise with the divine timetable.

In _The Way Of Christian Service_, we discussed this at length. The unconsecrated cannot wait for God. The carnal cannot wait for God. Those who want the approval of men cannot wait for God. There are God's deeds and there is God's time.

Your prayer has been heard. Your wife Elizabeth will bear you a son, and you are to give him the name John (Luke 1:13b).

The name was given by God. It was not the name of his relative. The name was given by God. Parents must wait on God and get the names of the children from God and give the names as prophetic acts

He will be a joy and delight to you (Verse 14a).

O that each son were a joy and delight to his parents!

And many will rejoice because of his birth, for he will be great in the sight of the Lord, he will be great in the sight of the Lord (Verses 14b-15a).

A son to be great in the sight of the Lord whereas you are preparing your child, not to be great in the sight of the Lord but to be great in the sight of the world. "He will be great in the sight of the Lord" – great in the sight of the Lord, destined to be great in the sight of the Lord "He will be great in the sight of the Lord." Is that what you are imposing on your sons, imposing on your daughters? Do you have an eye on your son becoming great in the sight of the Lord? Do you have a secret eye towards you son being great in the sight of the Lord? Great in the sight of the Lord! Great in the sight of the Lord! Great in the sight of the Lord! Great in the sight of the Lord! And great only in the sight of the Lord!

O you seek greatness! You yearn for greatness – but greatness before whom? You are bitter and jealous because you have no standing before men. But who can hinder you from being great before God—the only greatness that counts? Oh, "He will be great before the Lord! He will be great before the Lord! He will be great before the Lord!" We have the responsibility to build a career for our children that makes them great before the Lord!

We have the responsibility to strategise about careers for our children that will make them great before the Lord!

Mary F. is finishing in June - July. She is doing very well. She should have a minimum of an Upper Second. She wanted to go to South Africa to do a Masters and then a doctorate in Public Health. But a few months ago, the Lord said she should come back after her first degree to accelerate the writing of the Gospel. It's only now as I'm preaching that it just came to my mind. In the Colorado Springs Prophecy, "Your last daughter, Mary, will have a powerful teaching ministry. God will give her revelations and she will write many books." So, all of it holds together. So from July she'll be with us in the writing of books. There are many Public Health specialists. There are few writers of the Gospel.

"Great in the sight of the Lord, great in the sight of the Lord" – Is that your dream for your children or you want to give them all of the world and expect that they would be great before the Lord? May you repent of the corruption of your heart! May you repent!

I went to visit a leader in this city. He was not at home. His wife was there. I asked their little daughter, "What do you plan to be?" She said, "I will like to be a Nursery School teacher." Then her mother came out of one of the other room like a wounded lioness. She said, "Yes! Yes! Yes! Yes! Yes! That's you! That's you! Yes! Others want to teach at the University; you, Nursery School! Nursery School!" I have never felt like beating a woman like I wanted to do to her! That child will go wrong because of her mother. Again in this same city, I went to another home. There too was another girl. I asked her, "What do you want to do when you grow up?" She said, "I want to be a nurse." We were all in the same room. The mother turned, with eyes like those of a sorceress, she said; "Yes! You! Yes! Others want to be doctors; your own, nurse, nurse." Look at women, women, the wives of leaders who kill their children, destroy them and sacrifice them to the Devil. The glory of the world! The accursed glory of the world! The accursed glory of the world! The accursed glory of the world!

He will be great in the sight of the Lord, great in the sight of the Lord, great in the sight of the Lord. He is never to take wine or other fermented drink (Luke 1:15a)

– separated from the common, separated from the common. *He will never take wine or other fermented drink* – separated from the common.

He will be filled with the Holy Spirit even from birth (Verse 15b)

– filled with the Holy Spirit right from the womb!

Many of the people of Israel will he bring back to the Lord their God. And he will go on before the Lord, in the spirit and power of Elijah (Verses 16-17a).

Yes,

...He will go on before the Lord, before the Lord, in the spirit and power of Elijah, to turn the hearts of the fathers to their children and the disobedient to the wisdom of the righteous (Verse 17a,b)

The hearts of the fathers to their children and the disobedient to the wisdom of the righteous to make ready a people prepared for the Lord, and to make ready a people prepared for the Lord (Verse 17b,c).

Hallelujah! Hallelujah! Brethren, it's sweet, it's sweet. What a future!

Zechariah asked the angel, 'How can I be sure of this? (Verse 18a).

You want proof of what God has said. God has spoken; you want proof. May God rebuke your unbelief! May God rebuke your unbelief! May God rebuke your wanting signs so that you may believe! May God rebuke you who want external evidence so that you may believe what God has said to you! May God rebuke you who want the visible before you believe what God has said! May you repent of your unbelief that has not laid hold on what God has said, and wants small signs here and there so that you may hang on them! Zechariah wanted a sign. He got a rebuke and punishment! For the man of his standing, this might have been acceptable among the rank and file, but not for a spiritual General, for Zechariah was a general of God, wanting external evidence was not acceptable.

> *I am Gabriel. I stand in the presence of God, and I have been sent to speak to you and to tell you this good news. And now you will be silent and not able to speak until the day this happens, because you did not believe my words* (Luke 1:19-20a).

Because you did not believe my words, because you did not believe my words.

People do not go free for not believing God's words. For spiritual babes, it's alright, but for spiritual leaders, for spiritual leaders, for God's generals and God's colonels and God's majors and God's captains and God's lieutenants and God's field marshals, the higher you go, the more dangerous unbelief is. The punishment for unbelief is directly proportional to your position before God. The punishment is directly proportional to your rank. The punishment is directly proportional to your rank. The higher you go, the greater the punishment for unbelief. What God would ignore among the rank and file, the colonel, the general, the field marshal, will receive the severest punishment from God. Are you a general – full of unbelief as if you were a non-commissioned officer? Have you magnified the God who speaks to you?

I am Gabriel. I am Gabriel. I stand in the presence of God (Verse 19b)

– that is his rank.

I have been sent to speak to you and to tell you this good news. And now you will be silent and not able to speak until the day this happens, because you did not believe my words, which will come true at their proper time (Verse 19c-20).

He was made dumb because he did not believe.

It is not enough that a man is righteous! It is not enough that he keeps the Lord's commandments! It is not enough that he keeps the Lord's ordinances! He must be mighty in believing the Word of God! He must be mighty in believing the Word of God! He must be mighty in believing the Word of God! He must be mighty in believing the Word of God! He must believe the Word of God and he must believe what God is saying to him. He must believe what God is saying in the Scriptures and what God has said to him personally.

That's the preparation of a leader. So far, it depends on the parents - the roots, the roots, the foundation, the foundation!

What has God said to you about your children? What has God said to you about your children? What has God said to you about your children so that you are raising prayer unceasingly so that no word of the Lord concerning your child or your children would fall to the ground? You have been too lazy to go on retreat and wait and wait and wait until God speaks; and wait and go on the next retreat to wait and wait and wait until God speaks, so that you have the message of God for each child. And now you are guessing forward and backward. You have betrayed your children. You cannot tell them, "This is what God said," so that if they don't obey, at least you have spoken. You will not seek God for your children. You will not seek God for them so that you are bringing them up by gambling. You don't know what God has in mind therefore you cannot by prayer demolish what they have. That's one of the highest responsibilities that parents owe their children – to hear God clearly, to receive God's blueprint for the child and bring up the child according to that blueprint, praying that God would reveal things increasingly, with only one goal – that the child would be great before the Lord, so that you can say, "I have laid the foundation for a great child for God. I have fasted and prayed according to what I heard."

We are still on the message but we have just laid the foundation. We will come to John himself, the preparation of this man who shook the nation by his preaching.

LEADERSHIP BY DIVINE APPOINMENT

The Example of Noah

Leadership is by divine appointment; the example of Noah

Tuesday, 2nd January, 2007.

Spiritual leadership is by divine appointment. God appoints leaders! God appoints leaders! Say: "God appoints leaders!

"God appoints leaders!"

The first leaders that God appointed were Adam and Eve.

Genesis 1:26-30,

> *Then God said, 'Let us make man in our image, in our likeness, and let them rule over the fish of the sea and the birds of the air, over the livestock, over all the earth, and over all the creatures that move along the ground.' So God created man in His own image, in the image of God He created him; male and female He created them.*

> *God blessed them and said to them, 'Be fruitful and increase in number; fill the earth and subdue it. Rule over the fish of the sea and the birds of the air and over every living creature that moves on the ground.' Then God said, 'I give you every seed-bearing plant on the face of the whole earth and every tree that has fruit with seed in it. They will be yours for food. And to all the beasts of the earth and all the birds of the air and all the creatures that move on the ground - everything that has the breath of life in it - I give every green plant for food.' And it was so.*

This was the first appointment of a leader by God. The leader was created with a goal in view --

> *Let us make man in our image, in our likeness* (Verse 26a)

What for? Leadership is appointed with a goal in view! Leadership is appointed with a goal in view!

> *Let them rule over the fish; let them rule over the birds, over the livestock, over all the earth, and over all the creatures that move on the earth* (Verse 26b).

Leadership is appointed with a goal in view - a goal that the leader must understand very clearly and from which he may never depart. "Let us create man in our image"– for this purpose—for rulership over creation. Then leadership desperately needs the divine blessing - call it divine enabling. God blessed them. Hallelujah!

God gives the appointed leader the enabling! God never appoints a leader without giving him the enabling! God blessed! God blessed them! God blessed them! God blessed them! O, there is divine enabling! There is divine enabling! There is divine enabling! And for all, and for each one that God appoints to leadership. Leadership is not appointed so that it may function by its own self. Leadership is appointed so that it may function in the power of the divine enabling. God blessed them and God clarified their task.

- "Be fruitful,
- increase in number,
- fill the earth,
- subdue it,
- rule over the fish of the sea and the birds of the air and over every living creature."

It was very clear; very clear. But it doesn't end there.

God provides the needs of the leader.

Genesis 1:29,

> *Then God said, 'I give you every seed-bearing plant on the face of the whole earth and every tree that has fruit with seed in it. They will be yours for food.*

The leader's food is guaranteed. The leader's food is guaranteed by God, O, by divine provision. You can't lead people with a hungry stomach. You can't have someone with head with bones all over and who stands before people looking like a scarecrow and frightening the people. And if the people allow the leader to starve, they are answerable.

> *I give you every seed-bearing plant. Every tree that has fruit with seed in it will be your food* (Verse 29a).

The needs of the leader are guaranteed by the Appointer. God appointed, He blessed and He guaranteed the spiritual needs. He guaranteed the spiritual needs and He guaranteed the material needs.

And more than that,

> *And to all the beasts of the earth and all the birds of the air and all the creatures that move on the ground - everything that has the breath of life in it - I give every green plant for food* (Verse 30).

So the needs of the leader is provided for as well as those of the leader's household. God did not just provide for Adam; He provided even for the animals and the birds over which Adam was to rule. So in divine order,

- God appoints a leader,
- defines for him the spheres of his service,
- gives him divine enabling,
- provides for the leader, and
- provides for the leader's people.

It's beautiful. So we see there at the beginning of creation the divine order. In the provision of God, in Genesis 2:8,

> *Now the Lord God had planted a garden in the east, in Eden; and there He put the man He had formed.*

Taking care of the leader is a divine command.

Verse 9a,

> *And the Lord God made all kinds of trees grow out of the ground - trees that were pleasing to the eye and good for food.*

Good for the eyes, good for food. There's something here, brother. God gives the best to the leader − pleasing to the eyes, good for food. It is not the left-overs that are for the leader. It is the very best in everything. When the people of old wanted a wife for the king, what did they do? They searched for the most beautiful girl; didn't they? – Esther, Abishag. They were the most beautiful.

In the tribe of my father, women are classified into four groups. The most beautiful, and "beautiful" includes the physical and the character - "Beugha ayi Fon" – that's for the chief; second class beauty - "Beugha ayi Chinda" - that is, the king's servant; third class beauty - "Beugha Ayi ewie wereko" - that is for the wife of the common man. Fourth class beauty - "Beugha Ayi ewie ebogo" - that is the wife of the slave. Women were placed in four classes - the wife of the king, the wife of the king's servant, the wife of the common man and the wife of the slave. The best was for the king. It is in the divine prescription that the best be given to the king. Do you know why God does things that way? Because without leadership there is total confusion. So if there is no leader, there is total confusion. God's purposes cannot be accomplished without leadership. The leader must have the best so that he can concentrate on his sole responsibility of leadership. Say "Amen."

Let's move on to Noah. God had to wipe out the inhabitants in the world because of sin.

God wanted a new leader.

Genesis 6:8,

> *But Noah found favour in the eyes of the Lord.*

Noah found favour. Everything is by grace. Everything is by divine favour. But divine favour is not irrational. Say, "All is by grace.

All is by divine favour.

But divine favour is not irrational."

Genesis 6:9b,

> *Noah was a righteous man, blameless among the people of his time, and he walked with God.*

Why did Noah win God's favour? Why was Noah chosen to lead his generation? Why was Noah chosen to lead his generation? Why did he find favour before the Lord? — He was a righteous man, he was a blameless man among all the people of his time, and he walked with God - righteous, blameless and walked with God. He was righteous, he was blameless and he walked with God.

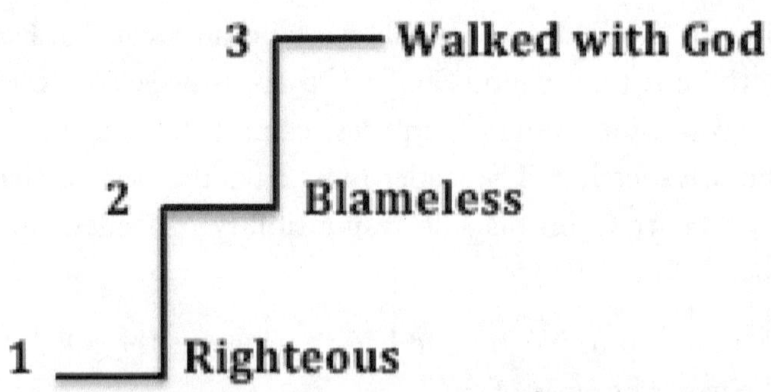

He was righteous, he was blameless and he walked with God. He walked with God. I want to tell you, divine favour is tilted towards the righteous, towards the blameless and towards those who walk with God! Divine favour is tilted towards the righteous, towards the blameless and towards those who walk with God! Therefore you can make yourself the object of God's favour. You can make yourself the object of God's favour by personal righteousness, by personal blamelessness and by a personal walk with God that satisfies the heart of God! You become the object of God's favour.

Again, Noah's sons are included because of the righteousness and the blamelessness and the walk with God of Noah. Look at the problems of your children, are they problems that are a consequence of your righteousness, problems in your blamelessness, problems that flow, and that flow from your walk with God or your wife's walk with God or both of you. It's a frightful thing. When you see a problem in your son or in your daughter, the first thing is to ask, "Is it not God exposing something wrong in my righteousness, in my blamelessness, in my walk with Him?" Could it be with your wife – a problem in her righteousness, in her blamelessness and in her walk with God?

Before you choose a partner, know that she will affect your children profoundly. So it's not just what you are. Your partner will affect your children profoundly. If one person is righteous and the other one is corrupt, they may reject the righteousness of the righteous and take only the corruption of the other partner.

It is said that Socrates was ugly, very ugly. There was a very beautiful woman in Athens. Socrates was very ugly but very intelligent. This woman was utterly beautiful and utterly stupid. So she went to Socrates and said, "Let's get married so that the children will have your intelligence and my beauty; they will be intelligent and beautiful or handsome." Socrates said, "You are just again manifesting your stupidity; suppose they take my ugliness and your stupidity so that they are ugly and stupid, what will they become?"

Oh, I am talking to the leaders of tomorrow. The girl you are bringing into your life, have you looked at the character that she is bringing along? The character of her father, the character of her mother, the character of her grandfather, the character of her grandmother, that's what will be found all over your house. Girl, the young man you are accepting, have you weighed his character? His character, his father's character, his mother's character, his grandfather's character, his grandmother's character − that is the packet that is coming along, and you shall see it in your children and in your grandchildren. You will not just see the physical; you will see the character. So when somebody knows, "I am a man of destiny. God has appointed me for consequential work," he will screen the partner because of what he will produce.

I cried one morning very much when Wesley described his marriage. He said he will live to regret it with all of his heart. And he said he believes his wife also regretted it with all of her heart. He said even when they were together, they were far apart. They were not together often but even when they were together, they were so far apart. A marriage that he contracted in his insanity! He violated the rules that they themselves set up for marriage. The marriage was to be approved by the brethren − all the marriages had to be. He asked no brother's opinion. He didn't even tell his younger brother. He was afraid that they will oppose it. They only heard that he had been married. For every tragic marriage, someone of consequence said "No," and many times. God never does a thing without warning His people. They were never divorced, but he heard about her death four days after she had died. And he expressed in his own words. He concludes it very differently. He said he has had very few things to regret in his life, and that the marriage was the central regret of his life. He said he didn't think that they ever loved each other but that even if they did, it lasted only a few months. Even true love can die. If true love can die, how much more that which was not love? People should reflect.

God be blessed; He gave them no children so the tragedy did not continue.

I have been working on some principles of guidance. One question that you should ask about the step you are about to take: "Who does not agree with me?" Write down the persons who are not in agreement with you and ask: "Are these people normally opposed to that which is right or are they people who oppose that which is wrong?" – Because for a man who normally opposes that which is right, his opposition needs not be considered. But if he's a man who opposes that which is wrong, you are in trouble.

Who else does not agree? How is he?

Thirdly, who does not agree?

Write down the names of those who don't agree and then make a list of those who agree then ask, "On which side is God?" If you want to go on a journey; who does not approve?

The whole world has suffered the loss of that marriage. God used Wesley exceptionally but this woman opposed him exceptionally. She was the widow of a merchant, the widow of a very rich man, used to ease, indulgence, luxury. And this fellow who at one point had only two silver spoons because he gave everything to God, what did he have to give this woman? He said, "One of the problems was that my poor wife was married to a man who was already married - married to a cause." Wesley was married to a cause. That was not a man for a woman to marry. This cause occupied him round the clock. It ate him, transformed him. Wesley travelled 250 thousand miles on horseback. He wrote or tore down 300 books. If you wrote a book that was nonsense, he wrote a book to tear down yours. It's difficult to think of a man who worked harder. Even at 84, he was still travelling 10 km a day to go and preach. There was no room for a woman. He was married to a cause. I want to advice those who are already married or who plan to be married to a cause to rethink.

Cowman (Charles), whose biography I've been quoting recently was completely sold out to his missionary call and so was his wife. His wife fitted into his life in all things. She wrote his biography. I think she was married to him to write that book! It's first class work. She is the author *Missionary Warrior*.

Pray that the people among us who should not marry, should not marry.

Are you married to a cause? Then you better stay single. Don't destroy another life. Imagine if the Apostle Paul were married. We must confront the fact that of the twelve Apostles, none who came to Jesus single got married. These were frontline men who were constantly on the move, constantly in peril, constantly in danger. Where could a home fit in their lives? Where could a wife fit in it? Where could children fit in? I want it known in heaven that I said this thing today. I want it known on the Throne so that the Wesleys of our generation might hear.

That C. T. Studd got married and saw his wife once in 13 years leaves us room to rethink. There are people who should renounce marriage for the sake of the call of God on their lives. Marriage means that there is time for the partner. So if one man is going this way and the other man the other way, the other man is going that way; disaster will result!

Some of you have read about Pastor Tsi. Sometimes husband and wife would meet on a lane in the forest, the wife coming from preaching in one direction, he going in the other. Then they would embrace each other. Sometimes when they managed to be at home, they would be so tired that they slept with their shoes and clothes on. We bless God, they didn't have children.

That's why we insist, brethren though demons oppose it — that until a man knows what God has called him to do with his life, he should not get involved with a woman. He should choose one according to the call of God on his life, not because he is burning. May God help us.

I want you to pray for your children that those who are not to be married should not be married. Protect their emotions. Smash all that the Enemy is trying to do to awaken love before time.

General Booth's daughter, had thirty-six offers from brothers for marriage. She turned all of them down and later became the fourth most powerful person in the Salvation Army worldwide. She went to France at the age of 19, hired a garage and began to storm from there until there were 5000 Salvation Army people there. And that was the day when the Salvation Army people knew radical consecration.

When you have a lioness who wants to marry some leopard, the leopard will suffer because a leopard is not a lion. There are girls who can shake you and throw you down. Some sister used to say, "I dislike dim-witted men." Such a girl should not marry.

On one mission field, when the couple was leaving for the mission field, they sold their house and kept the money. They decided to buy a taxi. They talked about it and the brother was to take the decision. He kept delaying action; by the third day his wife used the money for the house kept and paid for taxi. She took the money without telling the man and went and bought the taxi. The taxi broke down and they didn't get one franc out of it.

Don't go and ask them, "When are you getting married? When are you getting married?" Don't go and trouble the boys. There are some boys who are not interested in marriage. Sisters, don't go and awaken the love of such men. Don't cook food and take it to them. Don't woo them with your eyes to draw attention. Leave them alone.

Put your hands on your head.

Say,

> *"Lord,*
> *My choices will affect me profoundly.*
> *They will affect our children profoundly.*
> *They will affect our grandchildren*
> *   profoundly.*
> *My Lord,*
> *Smash every false choice of mine.*
> *Bring it to nought as a testimony of Your love*
> *   for me.*
> *My heart is prone to error.*
> *Come to my rescue, O God.*
> *Come to my rescue, O God.*
> *Come to my rescue, O God.*
> *Amen."*

LEADERS ARE GOD-APPOINTED

The examples of Abraham, Moses, the Kings, the Prophets and Saul of Tarsus

Tuesday, 9th January, 2007.

I want us to look at a number of examples of leadership. Leadership is God-appointed. Let's move on from Noah to Abraham.

Genesis 12:1-3,

> *The LORD had said to Abram, 'Leave your country, your people and your father's household and go to the land I will show you.*
>
> *I will make you into a great nation and I will bless you;*
>
> *I will make your name great, and you will be a blessing.*
>
> *I will bless those who bless you, and whoever curses you I will curse;*

and all peoples on earth will be blessed through you.

Abraham did not choose himself. Abraham did not choose himself. God chose him? When God calls a leader, there are some things that go with that call. But I want to say that God calls leaders not only to lead but in order that He might make them into great people.

"I will make you into a great nation. I will bless you!"

The call to leadership is a call to greatness according to God. It is a call to greatness according to God.

"I will make you into a great nation. I will bless you." The call to leadership is a call to blessings.

"I will bless you O, I will make your name great."

There are people who desire and are doing everything to make their names great. They want to make their names great.

"I will make your name great."

Listen, God is interested in making the names of men great! God is interested in making the names of people great! So if your task is to make the leader's name small, you are working against God.

"I will make your name great, and you will be a blessing."

Leadership is a call to provide the instrument through which God will bless others. It is a call to be a blessing, a call to be a blessing, a call to be a blessing – a blessing to oneself, a blessing to one's family, a blessing to one's neighbours, a blessing to those who are led!

"I will make you a blessing. ı will bless those who bless you."

Those who bless the leader are blessed by God. Those who bless the leader; who bless the God-chosen leader, are in turn blessed by God.

"And whoever curses you I will curse."

There are many people who bring curses upon themselves by cursing the leader, by rebelling, by resisting, by being indifferent and thereby bringing curses upon themselves. A wrong attitude to the leader is a curse upon the person. Listen, it was said of the Lord Jesus Christ,

> *This child is destined to cause the falling and rising of many in Israel* (Luke 2:34b).

In a sense, every leader is raised by the Lord; by people's attitude to him, they rise or they fall.

"I will bless those who bless you, and whoever curses you I will curse!"

Your wrong attitude towards a Leader is to your undoing! As you bless him you are blessed!

"And all peoples on earth will be blessed through you."

Abraham was a singular leader, destined to be an instrument of blessing to all peoples on earth. O but there is a sense in which every leader can bless every family that is on earth:

- by sacrificial gifts, money is released to ensure that all the families on earth hear the Gospel
- By radical praying, heart-cries are raised to the Lord so that each family on earth might hear the Gospel and be saved.
- By fasting, which is another way of crying out to God, the heart of God is moved, and the hand of

God is moved and released to bring blessings beyond our wildest imaginations.

I just did my budget, I've not been able to do so for the last month since I've been so mobile. This was just before me. I said to God, "I'm responsible for my family reaching every family on earth. Woe is me if I keep something that I could invest." Are you holding back what you ought to have invested to ensure that every family on earth hears the Gospel?

God chose Abraham. Abraham was chosen by God. Abraham - He led in a far-reaching way. As I think about it, I feel pain in my heart because Abraham was sent to the Promised Land. And when there was famine in the Promised Land, instead of Abraham staying in the Promised Land, he walked away from the Promised Land. Abraham was in the Promised Land, God was in the Promised Land, and there was famine in the Promised Land. And Abraham decided to move away from God in order to move away from the famine. And in Egypt you know what he found. He got Hagar from whom there are more than one billion people today. You know their attitude to the Lamb that was slain. Had Abraham not sought the security of this world, had he believed God and stayed in the Promised Land, the story would have been different.

Are you at crossroads? There are always these two pathways that we are talking about. Have you compromised so that you may live in comfort and miss God's best? My beloved, all hell is set out to ensure that you lower the standards you set. I see many young men, many young girls. They set out the standards for the person they want to marry. Later on, they ignore those standards completely and marry a wreck or a problem. They clearly said, "He should be this kind of person or he should be that kind or the other. After that, they ignore this standard and choose someone else. They close their eyes and choose for themselves. The result is the sad tragedies we call marriages today. Listen, you know what God first put in your heart. You know what God first put in your heart.

Let's come to Moses. Later on, we shall ask, "Why did God choose the people He chose?"

When it comes to Moses, first of all, there is a burning bush. An angel appeared to Moses and God called out to him. Listen to what God said.

Exodus 3:7-8b,

> *The Lord said, 'I have indeed seen the misery of my people in Egypt. I have heard them crying out because of their slave drivers, and I am concerned about their suffering. So I have come down to rescue them from the hand of the Egyptians and to bring them up out of that land into a good and spacious land, a land flowing with milk and honey...'*

Verses 9-10,

> *And now the cry of the Israelites has reached me, and I have seen the way the Egyptians are oppressing them. So now, go. I am sending you to Pharaoh to bring my people the Israelites out of Egypt.*

Moses had no such thoughts. The project was not his. God laid hold on him and God charged him. There are people who seek leadership for glory. That is a curse—the curse of seeking to lead for glory from man. Moses did not seek honour, glory, position. He did not seek leadership. God chose him. Moses was very reluctant. He was so reluctant to accept his appointment.

Exodus 4: 13,

... O Lord, please send someone else to do it.

You see, the Lord promised Moses all the miracles, all the greatness. Moses said, "Lord, send someone else." He had nothing to benefit from this promotion.

True leadership is suffering, suffering, suffering. It is being a target for blame 25 hours a day. If you take this decision, the people will oppose you. If you take the other, they will yet oppose you. Leadership is a call to give and give and give and give until nothing else is left. It's a call to suffer, suffer, suffer, and suffer. It's a call to be misunderstood, misunderstood, misunderstood, misunderstood, spoken evil of, spoken evil of, spoken evil of.

I read about a Pastor in America, who wrote in that his book. His church was a congregation of 200 people, everybody talked well of him. Then he caught the vision of church growth. It went to 2,500, 5,000, 10,000. Then every week there was something to write against him. The whole city now became angry. And he said, "And they have remained angry till today."

If you don't want people to speak evil of you, be a mediocrity, a failure or one of the common people. There's nothing to talk about them. O but dare to rise! Dare to rise! The higher you go, the more people will look for you to shoot.

In the book *Against the Tide*, all the opposition, all that was done and spoken against Watchman Née, the writer sums it up thus: "He who raises his head above others shall be shot."

Let me tell you a joke. It was told me by late Dr. Tutuwan. He said someone went to hell and was looking all over hell. They were in a very hot liquid that was burning them. Everywhere people were jumping, jumping for air and falling back, jumping for air and falling back. Then the person went to the quarter in hell where university teachers were, and there was absolute calm, no noise, no struggle. He said, "Because everybody was holding one another down so that no one could jump up. Therefore all of them were under."

Listen; if you are a mediocrity, people will have nothing to criticise. They have nothing to speak against. Nothing in you provokes jealousy. The criticisms will be proportional to your greatness.

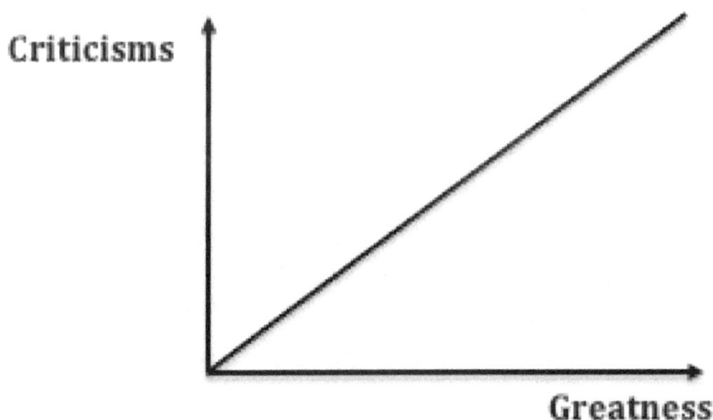

The greater you are, the more criticisms you will receive. The greater you are, the more you will be spoken evil of. The greater you are, the more your motives will be misinterpreted. The greater you are, the more you will be opposed. Moses did not want it but Moses led. And Moses led. Listen, God does not choose according to age. Aaron was older than Moses. God chose the younger brother. God does not appoint on the basis of age. It is not who came first into the Church that matters, God has other criteria. He has His own criteria for selection. Moses failed. Listen brethren, I've studied leadership for the last thirty years. The more I study it, the more I'm frightened. In the Bible, at least 80% of the leaders failed; it's a frightful thing.

Let me give a warning to you. If you choose to please the people instead of pleasing God, He will throw you away. If you give more time to being with the people instead of being with God, He will throw you away. God is the leader's choice. In fact, when a man is appointed a leader, the first thing is, he ought to weep. It's just like when a man is appointed treasurer. It's as if he has been appointed to fail in financial matters. Brother, most treasurers that I know in my life have failed financially, whether in the churches or in the work.

The leader is tested sorely. There are many things that others can do and go free. If you the leader do them, God will judge you immediately. There are things that others can do. If you do them as a leader, you will be done for. The others can compromise, if you do, you will be in hot water. Others can be disloyal; if you as a leader are disloyal, you'll be in the trouble of your life. Others can buy what they want; if you buy as they do, you'll be in trouble. The leader is under sealed orders.

In Numbers 28 Moses was disqualified.

Numbers 27:12-14a,

> *Then the Lord said to Moses, 'Go up this mountain in the Abarim range and see the land I have given the Israelites. After you have seen it, you too will be gathered to your people, as your brother Aaron was, for when the community rebelled at the waters in the Desert of Zin, both of you disobeyed my command to honour me as holy before their eyes.*

This was his first disobedience. He was disqualified.

Do you tremble about your call to leadership? Are you compromising? Are you saying, "Well, this person did it and went free. This person did it; went free. This brother is doing it. This sister is doing it"? You will be in trouble if you do it.

It takes only one disobedience and the leader may be put aside permanently. Errors that can be overlooked in the ranks and files, when the same are committed by the commander, are fatal.

There had to be a successor. It is not the duty of a leader to prepare a successor. I am very troubled. As I travel round the world, there are people who prepare their sons to take over the Ministry. If they don't have a son, they prepare a son-in-law. They want to keep it in the family – it is the case even in this city. The next leader is appointed by God and all succeeding leaders will be God-appointed.

Numbers 27:15-17,

> *Moses said to the Lord, 'May the Lord, the God of the spirits of all mankind, appoint a man over this community to go out and come in before them, one who will lead them out and bring them in, so the Lord's people will not be like sheep without a shepherd.*

Moses did not say, "O, I've been disqualified, I've been disqualified." He was not concerned about himself. He was concerned about what he was called to do, what God called him to do. God called him to take the people to the Promised Land. He was disqualified. His burden was that God might appoint somebody to ensure that they got to the Promised Land. Without the leader and the leaders, the Promised Land of God will not be entered into. There must be a shepherd. There must be a leader. Joshua was chosen by the Lord.

> *Take Joshua son of Nun, a man in whom is the spirit* (Numbers 27:18b).

The leader is chosen by God. At every moment the leader is God-chosen. Listen; Moses bowed to the divine choice.

In Deuteronomy 31:3 he says,

> *The Lord your God Himself will cross over ahead of you. He will destroy these nations before you, and you will take possession of their land. Joshua also will cross over ahead of you, as the Lord said.*

God ahead, the leader ahead. It is gross immorality to lead people who are ahead of you in their seeking of God, in their finding of God, in their knowing God, in their loving God. It's immoral to pretend to lead people who are ahead of you in the spiritual arts. It's immorality to pretend to lead people who know God more than you because you will be leading from behind. 'The Lord ahead of you, Joshua also ahead of you." When you stop being ahead, God will remove you or He may put you aside and allow you to play the buffoon before men. It is utter confusion when a person appointed to lead by God should through laziness, indulgence and self-sparing allow some of the people to go ahead of him. Then there can only be confusion. Ahead, ahead, ahead.

The same principle applies to all leaders. Let's come to the kings. The first king of Israel was God-chosen.

In I Samuel chapter 10 verse 24,

> *Samuel said to all the people, 'Do you see the man the LORD has chosen?*

"Do you see whom the Lord has chosen?" He was not the people's choice. He was the Lord's choice.

In I Samuel 15:27-28,

> *As Samuel turned to leave, Saul caught hold of the hem of his robe, and it tore Samuel said to him, 'The LORD has torn the kingdom of Israel from you today and has given it to one of your neighbours – to one better than you.*

The leader must make sure that he remains the best before God and before man. It is in God's purposes that the best leads. Through disobedience Saul was no longer the best. God found someone better than Saul. The leadership moved over to the one who was better.

In 1Samuel 16, the last part of the first verse, "I have chosen one of his sons to be king."

Who chose David? "I have chosen" – The Lord.

Verse 3,

> *Invite Jesse to the sacrifice, and I will show you what to do. You are to anoint for me the one I indicate.*

Verses 6-7a,

> *When they arrived, Samuel saw Eliab and thought, 'Surely the LORD's anointed stands here before the Lord.' But the LORD said to Samuel, 'Do not consider his appearance or his height, for I have rejected him.*

You can have all the qualifications before man but God will reject you.

Verse 7b,

> *The LORD does not look at the things man looks at. Man looks at the outward appearance, but the LORD looks at the heart.*

God chooses according to the heart. Verse 8b,

> *The LORD has not chosen this one either. Verse 9b, Nor has the LORD chosen this one. Verse 10b, The LORD has not chosen these.*

When David appeared, verse 12, the second part,

> *Then the Lord said, 'Rise and anoint him; he is the one.'*

God chose David. God chose David.

Let us look at the prophets.

Let us take Jeremiah, Jeremiah 1:5,

> *Before I formed you in the womb I knew you, before you were born I set you apart, I appointed you as a prophet to the nations. Verse 10, See, today I appoint you over nations and kingdoms to uproot and tear down, to destroy and overthrow, to build and to plant.* God-appointed, God-appointed.

In Luke 5:10b,

> *Then Jesus said to Simon, "Don't be afraid; from now on you will catch men."*

Peter was chosen by the Lord. Peter was chosen by the Lord.

In Acts 26: 16, the Lord said to Saul,

'Now get up and stand on your feet. I have appeared to you to appoint you as a servant and as a witness of what you have seen of me and what I will show you.' "I have appeared to you to appoint you..." In chapter 22 verse 10, *'What shall I do, Lord' I asked. 'Get up,' the Lord said, 'and go into Damascus. There you will be told all that you have been assigned to do.'*

Verses 14-15,

Then he said: 'The God of our fathers has chosen you to know His will and to see the Righteous One and to hear words from his mouth. You will be his witness to all men of what you have seen and heard.'

The leader is appointed by God. He is God-chosen. He does so by His divine prerogative. Of course, not every leader is chosen by God. With respect to the purpose of God, God chooses the leader.

We shall ask, "Why does God choose those He chooses?" This is because appointments are not done at random. He chooses those who satisfy His requirements.

Can you stand being spoken evil of—by the people closest to you, by those who ought to know better?

WHY GOD CHOOSES PEOPLE TO BE LEADERS

Why did God choose the people He chose?

The Cases of Noah, Abraham, Moses and Joshua

Tuesday, 16th January, 2007.

We are going to look at why God chooses people to be leaders. What qualifies them? The choice of leaders is a divine prerogative. God chooses spiritual leaders. He chooses them either because they are ahead of others in knowing Him and in loving Him or because they will be ahead of others in knowing and loving Him. I want to remind you that when you study the Bible, you will see that God calls man, God calls the believer to love Him with all of his heart. God calls believers to love Him with all their hearts and serve Him with all their might. Get that! Get that! Get that! God calls all believers to love Him with all their hearts and serve Him with all their might. That's why He gave you two legs –

one leg to remind you that you are to love the Lord with all your heart all the time, with all your heart all the time; the other leg – to serve Him with all your might. The question that you must immediately ask is, "Do I love the Lord with all my heart?" If you do not, you are a traitor. You are a traitor of God's call. "Do you serve God with all your might?" If you do not, you are a traitor to the basic call of God to be a child of His. God's choice of people to become leaders, He chooses the one who will love Him with all his heart all the time more than the rest, and the one who will serve Him with all his might all the time more than the others because, you cannot lead people who are ahead of you. If you do, you are a crook, a deceiver, a hypocrite, and God will throw you out or He may be using you just for some time to hold things together before the leader comes along.

The leader is ahead! The leader is ahead! Ahead! Ahead! Ahead! Ahead! And the people follow. If the people are ahead of him, he has lost his leadership because how will they follow? I want to tell you, the day the people overtake you, you have lost your leadership. The day one person goes ahead of you, the leadership changes hands. These are some of the factors that God takes into account when He chooses people for leadership.

We saw that God chose Noah. In Genesis 6:8 it says,

> *But Noah found favour in the eyes of the Lord.*

Why did Noah find favour? It was not incidental; it was not favouritism. The Bible says in Genesis 6:9,

> *This is the account of Noah. Noah was a righteous man, blameless among the people of his time, and he walked with God.*

Noah was ahead of the people. In fact, he was the only man like that. Noah was a righteous man! Noah was a blameless man! Noah walked with God! Why did Noah find the favour to be appointed leader? – By righteousness, by radical holiness, by blamelessness and by walking with God! That's what qualified Noah to be chosen to be the father of the next generation since God was going to wipe out all the rest. 'Righteous! Blameless! Walking with God!' And from the story, Noah was a workaholic! To have built this ark, to have called all the animals, to have identified the males from the females, their habits, what they would eat, and gathered all the materials and built this mighty ark required unusual abilities. An average worker would have failed. An above-average worker would have failed. It took extreme hard work to look for these animals and identify them; knowing how to catch them and how to keep them and how to nourish them required unusual abilities. God never picks a giant rat to lead. It's always an unusual man, always an unusual woman. But I tell you, it is the unusual in what depends upon a man, whether or not he has them. A righteous man — that was a matter of choice; wasn't it? A blameless man — that was a matter of choice. A walk with God was again a matter of choice. Then faith to believe God – Noah believed that what God had said would happen. You know "His Ambassadors" (choir) sang: "Noah has built himself an ark to sail it on dry ground." The power to believe God against the present evidence; the power to believe God when everything in the visible contradicts God's words. Faith! Faith! Faith! Faith! Faith! Faith! Faith! Faith is an indispensable attribute of leadership. A man who is moved by what he sees, if he is a leader, will be put aside because God calls leaders to believe Him when everything around them tells them there is no hope, when the evidence contradicts what God has said. The man must believe God about what God has said about him, and what God has said about his mission! And he must believe God that God is with him to start, continue and finish the project. There are many people who are mighty but they don't believe God. Therefore they cannot lead the people of God to do the near-impossible.

About obedience, God chooses people who will obey Him. In Genesis 6: 22,

Noah did everything just as God commanded him.

God must find in a man, or a woman with a commitment to obey the Lord, come rain, come shine. "Noah did everything just as God commanded him." God sees the future. He sees and asks Himself, "Will this person obey Me even if obeying Me puts all of him in peril?" Genesis 7:5,

And Noah did all that the Lord commanded him.

Do you have a commitment to obey God at any price? — To obey God when your obedience looks like foolishness? To obey God against logic, against security, against the visible evidence? Listen, are there things about which you must obey God today in order to put things right because you have slipped out of obedience? Things that you have allowed to slip off, in order to save yourself from being put aside? Faith is risking all on God, risking all on the promises of God. That was Noah.

Let's look at Abraham. Why did God choose Abraham? Again, Abraham was a man of might. O lazy brother, lazy brother, you have buried your leadership, you have buried your leadership! If you are not Number one in hard work, you have buried your leadership. When Lot was captured, Abraham took a personal army from his house – 318 men—

and smashed those kings and brought Lot back. May God deliver you from laziness! May God deliver you from laziness! May God deliver you from laziness! May God deliver you from laziness! May God deliver you from being the average! May God deliver you from being the average! May God deliver you from being above average! May God deliver you from accepting anything less than the all!

A personal army of 318 people raised in his house!

Some of you have heard me send people away from my house. I send people away from my house! If you are there, going nowhere, I will send you away! You may be very low but if you are committed to heights, you have a place. If you are just there going around in circles, if I keep you there, woe betide me. Gather all the people who have decided to go nowhere and fill your house with them. When the enemy comes, they will hand you over to him. Listen brethren; there were many people in our home some time ago. It was the time Mama Lydie (Sen) was ill. Brother Ernest Nzima came to spend time with Mama Lydie. They did not know he was there. He heard these people talking for four hours. At 6 o'clock the next day, he was back to the house. He told me, "The people you are keeping in this house can cut off your head. They are against you, they are against your message, against everything." Two of them were my wife's relatives. One of them was a student we had led to the Lord and had fallen out with his uncle who was paying for his studies. One of them was a sister who was going through a depression because she had lost her mother. These are the people who were talking and Ernest was hearing. The next morning, after Brother Ernest had talked to me, I decided that all of them would leave that same day or the next day. I gave one of them 80,000 francs to go back to Bamenda. One came and repented. I was stupid enough to have accepted the repentance. So the other three left. That one stayed, only to commit a major betrayal three years afterwards.

Whom are you keeping in your house? Our house is a training base for warriors. If you don't want to put your all to pursue the Lord you have no place there. Do they believe your message? Do they believe your manner of life? Do they share your vision? Are they prepared to make sacrifices?

Abraham built an army in his house. All about him was preparation for war and war. So Abraham was a man of might, a producer of people of might. He also believed God. He believed God. God told him, "I will make you into a great nation and I will bless you; I will make your name great, and you will be a blessing. I will bless those who bless you, and whoever curses you I will curse; and all peoples on earth will be blessed through you." (Genesis 12:2-3). He believed what God was saying. There was nothing to tell him that it would happen. There was no evidence. All that he had was what God had said. Verse 4a Genesis 12; "So Abram left, as the LORD had told him."

He was a man who could obey God by faith. Why did God choose Abraham? Genesis 15:6;

Abraham believed the LORD, and He credited it to him as righteousness.

Abraham would become a mighty intercessor. God knew that when He would ask for Isaac, Abraham would give Him Isaac, his one treasure on earth. God said, "Go and put an end to him." And he went away and he obeyed; bound the child, placed him on the wood, took a knife. You know what that means, brethren? Abraham had only one Treasure—God. Every other thing could go. Every other thing that he had could go. He was tested to the core of his being. Listen, Abraham was prepared to sacrifice even the promise of God to him on the altar of obedience. We say it again; Abraham was prepared to sacrifice everything on the altar of obedience, to sacrifice the son. Who could have understood him? – Nobody. And who could have stood with him? – Nobody. Had Isaac been killed, Abraham would have been left with nothing except God. That's why Abraham is the father of faith and a father to the faithful.

Let's move on to Moses. Why did God choose Moses? God does not choose giant-rats to lead the army of God. He does not choose mediocrities to champion major causes for Him.

Moses — it is difficult to think of a greater leader.

If you are chosen to lead a House Church of 40 people, the might that puts you ahead of those people will be required. If you are chosen to lead 400 people, the might that puts you ahead of those 400 people will be required. If you are chosen to take a city, the might required to take a city will be required of you. If you are chosen to take a region, the might required to take a region will be required of you. If you are chosen to take a nation and so on, a higher level of might will be required of you. If you are chosen to lead a House Church, little suffering will be required of you. If you are chosen to lead 400 people, more suffering will be required of you. If you are chosen to take a part of a city, still more suffering will be required of you. If you are chosen to take a city of 10.000 people, even more suffering will be required of you. If you are chosen to take a city of a million people or 10 million and so on, more and more suffering will be required, more and more sacrifice will be required because the leader is always ahead— ahead in suffering, ahead in sacrifice, ahead in being misunderstood, ahead in being spoken evil of, ahead in the number of people who hate him, ahead in the number of people who oppose him. And he takes it as part of his life. That he is spoken evil of is part of his cup of tea. That they build camps against him is part of it because as you know, 250 leaders of Israel stood up against Moses. The greater the man, the greater the opposition. When you look at the Bible, about the giants of giants, leaving the Lord Jesus aside, you see Moses, you see David, you see the Apostle Paul – leaders are in classes. What it takes to lead 10 people will not suffice to lead a hundred people because to be ahead of 10 people requires some effort. To be ahead of a hundred demands more. To be ahead of a thousand requires even more, to be ahead of 10 thousand, to be ahead of a million, to be ahead of 10 million all require unceasing degrees of suffering and sacrifice. The more people you have to lead, the more will be required of you. If you do not accept to embrace the cost, someone else will take over. You may think you are still leading but you are just the administrator because the leader is the one who is first before God. He is the Number one before God among the people he leads. When a person loses the power to be Number one, he may remain the official leader but God picks somebody else to replace him. Brother, you cannot lead from behind. Sister, you cannot lead from behind. You must ask, "What qualifies me to lead these people? What price have I paid to lead them? About what am I commanding them to follow?"

Look at Moses. First of all, he got to the heights of the world.

Moses got to the heights of the world – Acts 7:22,

> *Moses was educated in all the wisdom of the Egyptians and was powerful in speech and action.*

It was not a giant-rat that God chose to lead the children of Israel out of Egypt to the Promised Land - a man educated in all the wisdom of the Egyptians, all the wisdom of the Egyptians, and he was mighty in his speech. Oh, he knew how to communicate, how to move people through talking! And he was mighty in his deeds. He did not get there by chance. There's a song, *Cadeau (Gift); Eh! Cadeau! – Everything cadeau. Everything, cadeau.* Oh; you are deceiving yourself! You are deceiving yourself! You are deceiving yourself! It's not 'cadeau.' It's not 'cadeau.'

O Brethren, I am reading the seventh biography of John Wesley. I want to tell you brother, unless you put in your all, God will throw you away! Sister, I want to tell you, unless you put in your all and continue to put in your all, God will throw you away! Let me just tell you two things from the book. His brother and he, for a long period, didn't eat meat for years because they needed to save money to feed prisoners. They were doing everything to give what they could to prisoners. For years, they didn't drink tea, they didn't drink coffee. They took some leaves that were cheap and boiled them and drank the brew. He said he bought old clothes and adjusted them. He said he could not change his clothing, could not modify his life while there were starving people in Britain. For a period of 50 years, he lived on 30 pounds a year. As the prices went up, he reduced what he had. He lived on the harshest, barest minimum in order to support their Ministry and in order to give to the poor. There was a time they ate only bread because they saw these prisoners – starving. How could they live comfortably? For his tax declaration one year, he said he had only two silver teaspoons.

You want to live in luxury. You will never be great for God while people are going to hell whom you could rescue from hell if you gave up your luxury and gave the money saved to the cause of the Gospel!

As a Junior Fellow (Assistant Lecturer) at Oxford, his salary was 60 pounds. He lived on 28 and gave 32 away. When he became Senior Fellow (Senior Lecturer), his salary doubled to £120. He continued to live on £28 and gave 92 pounds away. Since he wrote many books, when he got a thousand pounds, he continued to live on £28 and gave this (972 pounds) away.

$$60 \quad 120 \quad 1000$$
$$\underline{28 \quad 28 \quad 28}$$
$$32 \quad 92 \quad 972$$

May God trouble you this day and trouble you about the indulgence of your life and your aspiring to leadership! May God trouble you! May God trouble you! May God trouble you! May God trouble you, trouble your wife, trouble everybody in your house about your indulgence when 10 francs can save someone! May your conscience be troubled! May the Holy Spirit wage war on your conscience! May the Holy Spirit wage war on your conscience! And may the Holy Spirit wage war continuously, unceasingly, in increasing intensity on your conscience!

I was saved by a tract. If that tract never came, maybe I would have missed that hour of salvation. Maybe the devil would have taken over and hardened my heart so that I never respond; because people do not just believe because they hear the Gospel rather, they believe because they heard the gospel at the opportune moment, when their hearts were tender. I want you to get that, brethren. People do not just believe because they hear the gospel. They believe because they heard the gospel at that time when their hearts were prone to believe. When that time passes, they may hear a thousand sermons and never believe. That is the tremendous responsibility of the person who postpones what he should give, who plans to give in the future when he ought to give today, who plans to sacrifice in the future instead of doing so today.

Again I want to bless those who pray for me because the Holy Spirit guides my reading in a way that baffles me. After the biography of Charles Cowman; it was imperative that I read the book I am reading now. I would have missed it; I would have missed what was the cry of my heart. Thank you very, very much for praying. When I got to Benin, Wilfred Lekunze came from Ghana and gave me that biography. I have read many biographies of John Wesley but this one is written to show why God used him. So the man goes into depths that other people don't talk about.

Moses was well-educated in all the wisdom of the Egyptians and was mighty in his words and in his deeds. But lest he should count on worldly wisdom, (this period of education in all the wisdom of the Egyptians and his might in word and deed) God now sent him to the University of God where he spent 40 years learning to die to self.

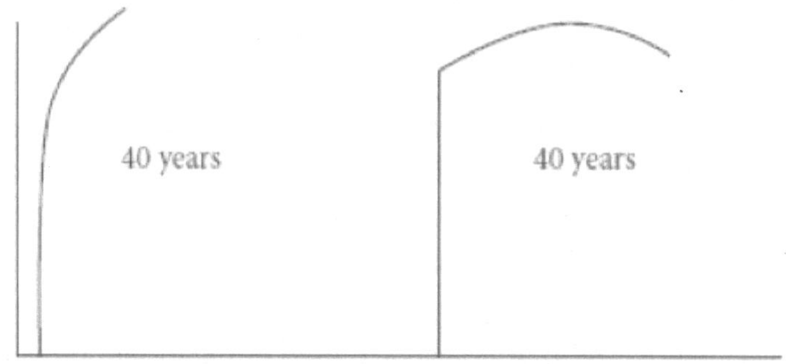

He had gone so high in the world that, if God had sent him, he would have counted on worldly wisdom, worldly analyses, a worldly way of thinking. God took him for 40 years and reduced him to nothing, gave him sheep to take care of, not his own sheep; so he had nothing to boast about. If you come from the tribe where my father comes from, to be the servant of your father-in-law is not honourable. They will ask you, "Are you bewitched? But that's the office that they gave him—to serve his father-in-law. When the sheep grew in numbers, the honour went to Jethro not to Moses. When one of the sheep was torn, Moses was held to blame. The University of God! The University of God! If you are not a servant of man, you will never be a servant of God. Moses spent 40 years learning how to serve man – how do you let the honour for all you do go to some other man while all the blame for all that goes wrong is cast upon you. If you don't have a heart disposed in that direction, you will not go very far in leadership. You will fail in the University of God. If you want to start with your own greatness, God will tear you down and throw you away. For 40 years, Jethro's flock, Jethro's flock, Jethro's flock, Jethro's flock, Jethro's flock. Look at Moses before the flock: "Sheep, your shepherd was educated in all the wisdom of the Egyptians!"

Response from the sheep: "Meee, meee, meee."

"Sheep, your shepherd was mighty in speech and deed!" "Meee, meee, meee." "Sheep, your shepherd was handsome, was greatly admired!" "Meee, meee, meee." That's all that worldly accomplishments serve for – for nothing, absolutely nothing, absolutely nothing in the service of God. Forty years – learning that all that he had acquired in Egypt had no place, no contribution to make in the service of God. After 40 years he graduated. You know the degree he got? "I AM NOBODY. I AM NOTHING." God told him, "I will do this through you. I will do this through you. I will do this through you." It did not excite him. The glory of the world had lost the power to excite him. The praise of men had lost the power to excite him. You know what he told God. "Send somebody else to go and do these great things." He was now ready. Then God called him and God used him. You see, brother, in every situation that came forth, Moses asked God. It was: "God said to Moses, God said to Moses, God said to Moses." He could not appeal to his learning. He had died to that. He could not appeal to the world, to worldly methods, to worldly thinking. He had to hear God and do what God said.

I want to say brethren, that this is the greatest plight of the leadership in Yaounde. One of the leaders told me. "If I have to wait and hear God before I act, I may never act." It was one of the most wicked words I ever heard because he's continually going and doing many more things for us according to his thinking.

Listen, my beloved, those miracles that Moses did, how could his worldly might have helped him? – In nothing. Will your degrees bring about darkness? Will they bring forth the locusts? Will they produce a snake that will swallow the snakes of the Egyptian magicians? Will your honour, your position, and all that, bring down the destroying angel? Will your connections, your bank account and all that, cause God to send the wind that divides the Red Sea? Will it rain down manna? Will it send quails and so on? Will it show the way through the desert? There were about three million people and there was no doctor for 40 years. Their shoes neither wear out nor did their clothes.

May God tell us. May He write on our hearts. May He trouble us beyond measure that the leadership of the people of God is according to the Rhema of God and that until God speaks, to act is treason and that after God has spoken, not to obey is treason.

God found a man big enough to forget his greatness and to lead a people who, all they did was to speak evil against him yet to be an intercessor for them.

Joshua was the next leader, and Moses and he have one story. The whole of the story of Moses is a very painful one. But look at the man.

Deuteronomy 34:10-12,

> *Since then, no prophet has risen in Israel like Moses, whom the LORD knew face to face, who did all those miraculous signs and wonders the LORD sent him to do in Egypt – to Pharaoh and to all his officials and to his whole land. For no one has ever shown the mighty power or performed the awesome deeds that Moses did in the sight of all Israel.*

We have spoken of Moses for long. There's a big volume written on leadership in the style of Moses which we wrote many, many years ago, *Leading God's People*. We had two Leadership Courses in Obili on Moses. You see, the greatness of Moses was twofold—It was an unusual knowledge and an unusual relationship with God and then unusual service.

Let me make you know that my relationship with the Lord is my primary preoccupation. Serving the Lord is only secondary. My inward journey to lay hold on God, to know Him, to possess Him, to be possessed by Him and to give Him my all is the central issue of my life. It's what I pursue relentlessly. When I went to Mont Febe in 1977 and spent four days there until God appeared to me, it had nothing to do with service. In Kampala in 1971, I woke up on a Saturday morning and I was boiling to pray; I felt that if I didn't pray I would break. I went to a lecturer's flat who was on holiday and had left his keys with me and began to pray there at the top of my voice. One brother, James Subuga came and knocked at the door. He too had a key. He said I was disturbing and I just told him to go away quickly. It was good that he just left. I continued to pray until I was carried out of this life for six hours during which before the Throne of God I learnt intercession. It had nothing to do with service. I want to confess that my heart hungers for God. My heart hungers for God. I hunger for God. It has nothing to do with service.

I want to plead with each leader to seek God, to seek God, to seek God and to keep seeking God and to keep seeking God and to keep seeking God and to major in seeking God and to major in finding God, to know God, to love God and to make Him your bliss.

Last year, Prisca and I gave God 39 million 660 thousand francs. It has nothing to do with leadership. It has nothing to do with normal income. This year, we'll give Him 50 million. That's what I've been given faith to lay hold on. It has nothing to do with leadership, I've sold the clothes that Robinson and Elizabeth sent to us, and I've sold the things that were bought for me in India when I went there. I still have things to sell. I have two very beautiful Samsonite suitcases. I've sold books. I have one pair of shoes—this one. And I will never have two while people are perishing and we don't have money for tracts. It has nothing to do with leadership. It has to do with the fact that shortly after the Holy Spirit came upon me, I was taken to hell and I saw the agony of people in hell. In fact, I was first taken to hell before I was taken to heaven. In 1985, I had been preaching the Gospel in Cameroon for 10 years. I locked up myself in that room which was my Retreat Room in Nkolbisson[1]. I was asking God to speak to me in the light of 10 years of preaching the

Gospel in Cameroon. I was fasting. I was locked in. On the sixth day, God spoke to me for six hours. I was writing on cards as He was speaking. The Lord asked me, "How much of your world's goods did My Highly Exalted Son possess when He was in your world?" He asked me the question and kept silent. And I know how much the Lord had. Then He said to me, "Go and possess what He possessed. Go and possess what He possessed." How much did He possess? Then He said to me, "Give Me an opportunity to spend My vast resources, resources that will be useless at the return of My Most Highly Exalted Son. Give Me an opportunity to spend My vast resources, resources that will be useless at the return of My Most Highly Exalted Son." When the Lord Jesus Christ comes, all the treasures of the earth will be useless to God. The only thing that can be useful for God is what is sent into the treasury of God now that can be used for the saving of the lost or for the perfecting of the saints. I understood from what the Lord said that there is a time factor involved; things that are not sent up urgently will lose their value because when He comes they will be meaningless. In order to give Him an opportunity to spend His vast resources, I must by my own life tell Him that I believe Him. I believe God about money. I believe God about investing money in the perishing souls of men.

I want to invite every leader and every would-be leader to specialise in knowing God, to specialise in knowing God. I want to beg you, my brother; I want to beg you, my sister, seek God, find God, know God, love God, serve God, let God be your Treasure.

Since then, no prophet has risen in Israel like Moses, whom the LORD knew face to face (Deuteronomy 34:10).

It was knowledge. It was the relationship. Moses said to God, "Show me now Your glory." Exodus 33: 18,

Now show me Your glory.

God said, "Now, go, you will succeed without Me." Moses said, No.

If Your presence does not go with us, do not send us up from here (Exodus 33:15b).

Are you seeking success or are you seeking God? Can you have godless success? Moses wanted God. He went to the mountain alone with God, alone with God, alone with God. But he also served God unusually. Unusual knowledge of God and unusual service of God are two sides of the same coin. But I call you to specialise in knowing God and God will flow out in your service to Him. Moses knew God. God knew him and God worked in him and through him. He was ahead of all the people in the knowledge of God.

He was ahead of everybody in obeying God. And God's power flowed through him in an unparalleled way.

But Moses failed. I want to say it was painful to know that God had perceived this failure and therefore gave Moses a limited commission. In Exodus 3 verses 7-10 the Lord said,

I have indeed seen the misery of My people in Egypt. I have heard them crying out because of their slave drivers, and I am concerned about their suffering. So I have come down to rescue them from the hand of the Egyptians and to bring them up out of that land into a good and spacious land, a land flowing with milk and honey - the home of the Canaanites, Hittites Amorites, Perizzites, Hivites and Jebusites. And now the cry of the Israelites has reached Me. and I

> *have seen the way the Egyptians are oppressing them. So now, go. I am sending you to Pharaoh to bring My people the Israelites out of Egypt.*

He didn't add, "And to bring them to the land." He knew Moses will fail so he had a limited commission because the task of bringing them into the Promised Land was to devolve on another. Normally, change of leadership is through death. Moses could have continued. It was not a matter of years. The people could rebel many times but the one rebellion of Moses was fatal. If you are a leader and you measure yourself by the people you lead and you listen to them and compromise and become understanding, you will be eliminated. Moses could not say, "Well, I've never disobeyed You before God. The leader cannot afford one act of disobedience. It could be fatal. For Moses it became a sin unto death. I want to tell every leader here, I bring you a warning from God. The next sin you commit knowingly may be your last time on earth. Leadership is a frightful calling. You have planned some sin, you have planned some disobedience, planned something that God has not approved, planned something that God has not called you to. I want to beg you now and beg you in the name of the Lord! Don't do it.

Everybody who is overweight or obese is an offence to God! You are a glutton! God does not look at just the spirits of people; He looks at their bodies. I have the scale drawn by the Diabetic Federation. Someone like Joe Besong is just a normal person. If Marie Mbock puts on 3kg she'll be overweight. So most people are deceived. Dr. Njamen is going to produce the scale and sell it so that people may know because there are so many people deceived. They are obese but they don't know it. My beloved, I beg you, do something about it. Do something about your weight.

I have promised God I will not go into next year without bringing my weight to a maximum of 65kg. That is the maximum weight. He told me I should start the fast at 65kg and end at 55kg. It is when I got the table from the Diabetic Society that I found that for 1 metre 72, my weight should be 65kg. And God has said I should go between this and 55.

1 metre 72 => 55kg — 65kg

God certainly knows the weight that is best. I saw the table not long ago but God had said it to me long ago. I was provoked by John Wesley. He was 5 feet tall. But I want to say that he weighed 122 pounds. It is about 58, 59kg, and after 10 years he still weighed 122 pounds.

122 pounds —> 122 pounds

And when he was 84, he walked 6 miles to go and preach.

You are responsible for all the light that God has shown you. I beg you, great deeds done for God and great sacrifices for God will not save you from being judged by God if you deliberately disobey. God did not spare Moses. God did not say, "This man has done so well in the past." Every moment is the determinant moment for a leader. Every moment is the determinant moment for the leader. Failure to obey God now may be disastrous beyond telling. Don't take a chance. I beg you. I plead with you as I plead with myself. That may be the fatal disobedience.

Pray that every leader here would tremble
before God.

Pray for me that neither now nor in all the

> *future would I knowingly disobey God in
> anything because it could be the end.*

> *Pray that I would never listen to man at the
> expense of what God has said to me and
> so fail Him.*

Lastly, the bank of heaven and the treasury of heaven and all the other accounts of the Triune God have been revealed to me.

> *Pray that I would render to God the reckless
> obedience that will qualify me to handle
> those accounts, draw from those accounts
> as a preview, as a foretaste of the coming
> Glory.*

If you don't understand it, just pray in tongues.

Moses was only temporarily disqualified. He did cross over into the Promised Land. In fact, he entered with a promotion. You see him on the mountain with Elijah and the Lord of glory. Had he crossed before, he would not have seen the Lord's pre-resurrection glory. But there the Lord was transfigured before him.

If you have failed in the past, repent and run after God with all your heart. He will have mercy on you and, even through your failure, promote you.

WHY GOD CHOOSES CERTAIN PEOPLE—JOSHUA

Why does God choose certain people to become Leaders?

Tuesday, 23rd January, 2007.

W hy does God choose certain people to become leaders?"

People are chosen for what they already are and because of what they will become. Let's look at the example of Joshua. Why was Joshua chosen to continue the leadership that Moses left? There were many people who could have been chosen but why was it Joshua? Joshua was chosen because he could continue the leadership that had been provided by Moses. God had led Moses. He had commanded Moses and had instructed Moses. He had taken Moses and the people so far in the direction of what was shown him on the mount. If the person who took over wanted his own programme, his own methods, it would have been disastrous. God would have had to start all over. So God chose a man who was committed to the Mosaic vision from his heart, who had no vision of his own.

It is not possible that God calls a man to continue, who is not interested in the vision He has already given, and who is not committed to it from the heart. Brethren; it's a very serious matter. If your heart is disloyal, that is, in the depth of it, at that level which only God knows, to the leader who is there with you, God will never make you the next leader because there will be confusion. God weighs the heart.

I've spent three years now studying the Revival of the 19th century. Last year, I read two volumes, each over 600 pages, on George Whitfield. And I read them within 10 days—so 1200 pages and more, because there's a coming Revival, a global Revival. I have some part to play in it. Our Ministry has some part to play in it. I've just finished reading the seventh book on John Wesley. Whitfield started the Revival and Wesley continued it. You will find that a disloyal heart, the power to think differently, is your worst handicap. I'm reading about the Welsh Revival. But before the coming Revival, we are going to have a Revival in our own Ministry. God is looking at the heart. The one who cannot be loyal to man cannot be loyal to God. If you cannot be loyal to man whose heart is not very different from yours, how can you be loyal to the Almighty God? If you cannot follow a man, how can you follow the invisible God? If you cannot follow a human leader from your heart, only demons can deceive you to think that you can follow the Almighty God.

Joshua was Moses' servant. That was his popular name – Joshua, the servant of Moses. Whose servant are you? If not, you are a rebel and you will lose the best that God has in store for you.

We already saw that slaves of men have the best position in heaven, servants of men are great, and there is no place there for bosses. The fact that you have not undertaken to be a servant of a man, neither can you become God's servant. You may be deceived. Joshua was Moses' servant. You know when Moses was called to the mountain to be shown the heavenly pattern of the tabernacle, Joshua was not called. Only Joshua went up too because he was Moses' servant. God was talking to Moses, Moses, Moses, Moses, Moses, Moses, Moses. Since Joshua was the servant, when Moses went up the mountain, all the rest were told to stay behind. All the leaders were told to stay behind. Joshua alone went along with Moses. Exodus 24:1-2,

> *Then he said to Moses, 'Come up to the LORD, you and Aaron, Nadab and Abihu, and seventy of the elders of Israel.*
>
> *You are to worship at a distance, but Moses alone is to approach the LORD; the others must not come near. And the people may not come up with him.*

So Moses and the seventy leaders all got to a certain point. Verses 9-10,

> *Moses and Aaron, Nadab and Abihu, and the seventy elders of Israel went up and saw the God of Israel. Under His feet was something like a pavement made of sapphire, clear as the sky itself.*

They went as far as the place where they could see the feet. That's what they saw of God. That's what God allowed them to see. There's what everybody can see. There's what a select group of leaders can see. But there are far-reaching heights of God, and people are admitted to how far they may go. So Moses, Aaron, Nadab and Abihu and the seventy went as far as they could see the feet of the Lord. Verse 11b, *They saw God, and they ate and drank.*

Verse 12,

> *The LORD said to Moses, 'Come up to me on the mountain and stay here, and I will give you the tablets of stone, with the law and commands I have written for their instruction.*

The command was given to Moses, "Moses, come." We see something far-reaching in verse 13. Verse 13a,

> *Then Moses set out with Joshua his aide.*

It is his "servant" in the original version of the Bible. It is only this modern version that says 'his assistant.' The modern man cannot understand 'the servant.' God told Moses to come. He went along with his servant.

Whose servant are you – so that when God calls that person to the extraordinary, you may come under his cover and God will accept you?

I'm desperately in need of a servant. Brethren, listen, let me speak a bit from the bottom of my heart. I did the 52-day Fast. At those heights I was alone. This fast will be unusual. I've been told to extend it to 56 days because there will be a Joint Service at Damase Centre on the 56th day. That's the day our whole Ministry worldwide will gather. All the people in our Ministry worldwide are going to gather in different places for the Holy Spirit to come upon us. Though supra-long fasts end at 55 days, God has asked me to spread out onto that day as an exceptional measure because that's the day He will visit the Work. He has promised me I will be strong and running on that day. It is because of the whole matter of territorial spirits, and now hosts of wickedness in heavenly places. I seek a servant to go with me into this so that though not called to supra-long fasts, he might be given the enabling because he's under my cover in order that there may be someone apart from myself with intimate knowledge about territorial spirits, then about hosts of wickedness in heavenly places. But he must be a servant. He must be my servant. He has to have the spirit of a servant and the disposition of a servant. As I look ahead, it is very deeply troubling, brethren, because when we get to the tenth supra-long fast, one person ought to go to Varanasi, one person to the headquarters of Hinduism and one person to the headquarters of Malsi to proclaim the victory. I don't know what God will have to do but the attitudes of people could block God's planetary programmes because God has chosen to co-work with us. He could work without us but He has chosen not to. I believe with my whole heart that there are two brothers here who were sent to be my servants by the Lord but they chose not to be. As I see the fact that the destiny of 4.5 billion people is at stake, as I begin to wonder that only one place will be represented out of three, what will be the impact on the whole battle? I believe it with all my heart because about this conflict with the hosts of wickedness in the heavenly places, the Lord said to me, "It's not a battle to which I said whoever would do it, let him come; and then I sent the person who was available. I have called you personally to do it. If you don't do it, it will not be done because I will not call somebody else to do it." My Joshuas also refused. Sometime in the years past, they must have received a specific call from God to come and be my servants and they turned it down. Or maybe God called them to pay the price that would qualify them to serve me and they refused. God might have told them to do something and they chose to compromise. Compromise! Maybe it was the thought of the pain that they were going to experience, pain!

Did you compromise in order not to feel more pain? Did you compromise in order not to feel more pain, in order to save yourself from anguish, to save yourself from obeying even when you did not understand? But compromise leads to comfort. You compromised and therefore you felt at ease: and then to being a mediocrity.

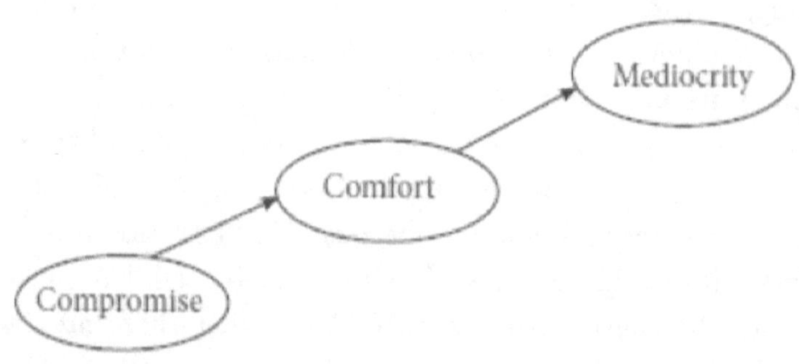

That's the lower pathway that John Wesley talks about. Did you compromise? My brethren, so often, the Lord has placed two pathways before me. Sometimes He has spoken to me today and the next day given me a message that freed me in order that I should beg Him to give me the painful way because He would not force anyone. There's always a choice. You can compromise. You can compromise. At the point of compromise you settle in comfort. The long-term consequence is that you will become a mediocrity. Or you could choose sacrifice, self-denial, suffering and glory.

Brethren, everyday – maybe now as never before, I see two pathways almost in everything—two pathways, two pathways, two pathways. I faced one of the pathways at a moment in the fast when I had malaria, malaria, malaria. I've taken three malaria drugs, three different malaria treatments during this fast. At some point, the Lord told me, "Stop it. Go and evangelise. There's a world perishing." And I saw what I could do without the Fast, had it not been that in Canada the Lord had said to me, "The dismantling of these hosts is given to you, Zacharias Tanee Fomum. I've given it to nobody else. If you don't do it, I will give it to nobody else." In the crisis of my pain and battles and the release from the fast as I received, what kept me going on and not to accept the release was the fact that if I don't do this supra-long fast, since there's a time limit, I would have failed totally.

Listen, my beloved; you too may stand at similar crossroads. It may not be linked to the fast. It may be with some other issue. There are some exams with God that if you fail you can come and do again. There are others that when you fail, it's over. There are no repeats. Maybe you don't know how consequential you are. Maybe you don't know how consequential you are!

We are in our year of decision. Brethren, we are near a major breakthrough. If you are going out of Yaounde now, let God sign it seven times. Your loss may be beyond telling. It may be eternal. Can you imagine somebody who was not in the Upper Room on the day of Pentecost? You know their Pentecost was different from the others. I beg you, stay in the city. If you are going for two, three days and God signs it seven times, go but rush back. Go, and rush back. Yaounde is determinant with regards to what God will do very soon. If there was ever a time when people should pray without ceasing in this city, it is now. If there was ever a time when people should pray without ceasing in this city, it is now. If there was ever a time when people should fast and fast and fast in this city, it is now. Those of you who stopped, as soon as you strengthen yourself a little, join the fast. If there was ever a time when you should strip yourself of all sin, it is now. If there was ever a time when you should get right with God, it is now. If there was ever a time when your most cherished idol should go, it is now. If there was ever a time for you to lie flat before God and cry out to Him to give you His best, it is now. If you love your people, gather them unto the Lord. Help them to strip off all that must be stripped off. Help them to repent as they have never repented before, to abandon sin as they have never abandoned, to carry out restitutions even if it breaks the heart. I don't know when, but God is going to do very deep things.

I told a brother yesterday, "Work on your heart because something seems to move you out at the moment when God is about to do something great." We had the last Prayer Crusade that went on for 70 days. We had planned it to stop on the 71st day but on the 70th day God dramatically brought it to an end. This brother who had been there all through, went out of the hall about two hours before the event in order that he might miss it. Yesterday morning, there was another determinant moment. He also went out just before. I told him, "Work on your heart. Work on your heart. Work on your heart. There's something working against you to make you miss that which you should be part of."

The real way not to lose out is that you put your plans aside, your wisdom aside; and what God commands you, do. Then you can never miss it. To succeed, you ought to have been severed from logical thinking and natural affections, and want only one will – the will of God. You seek only one will—the will of God. To seek God's will, you have to live exclusively for God's pleasure. If you are living for the pleasure of God and your pleasure, you will miss it. If you live for God and for your family, you will miss it. If you live for God and for your Ministry, you will miss it. If you live for the exclusive glory of

God, for God's will alone, for what will please God alone, you will not miss it. I beg you, rush into the arms of the Lord, cling to Him and tell him, "God, don't let me depart." Do it right now.

People do not forge ahead because they can. You go ahead because there is no other way. You know in Lagos, brethren, a brother and a sister collapsed on the 36th day of the fast. Nevertheless, they woke up and completed the fast. It was war with their families, their families in the flesh, I'm not talking to children, I'm talking to spiritual adults. There are those "If I perish, I perish" situations. Our body is open to the Enemy's attack. The Enemy attacks from outside; so the first target is the body. If you don't learn to laugh at his intrigues ... I'm saying this for the instruction of the saints for the future. We have our strengths. Failure where our strength lies has very far-reaching consequences. And it is in the Enemy's strategy that we should fail in these.

Abraham was the man of faith. When he turned to another woman in unbelief, he got Ishmael and there are more than one billion Ishmaelites today, nearly impossible to win, the product of the faithlessness of a man of faith.

Listen brethren, we are in our most determinant battle. The time before us will make or mar this city. Because I must be at Damase and end the fast in Damase on the 4th of March, you can start the fast tonight; it will be 40 days to that day. So there is still an opportunity for someone who compromised, who took a decision on the basis of compromise; he decided on how long he must fast on the basis of compromise. To redeem the situation, – Sacrifice, suffering, greatness; self-sacrifice, suffering, greatness/glory – this is another pathway.

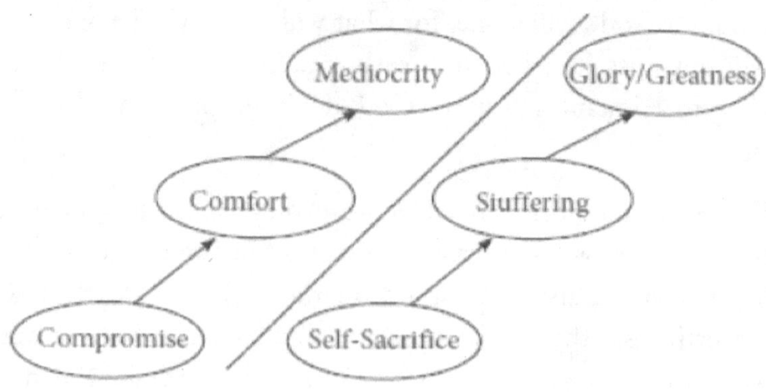

Brethren, the temptation to compromise is very, very, very, very frequent, very frequent, very frequent! Are your fiercest temptations in the area of money? Are your greatest temptations in the domain of the opposite sex? Are your greatest temptations in the area of self-glory? Howbeit, there's also the presence of the Holy Spirit within whispering to you, "My son, my daughter, this is My way, walk in it."

The Lord had said to us that at Etoug Ebe we no longer have Prayer Nights. What we had were Prayer Mornings from midnight to 6 a.m. in the morning. We went back to starting at 10. The Prayer Nights at Etoug Ebe will start at 10 p.m. even if there is only one person there. He must start to pray at 10p.m.. This starting time must never be altered for any reason. For the Thursday nights, there is already Prayer there so that even if it starts later, it's not a Prayer Morning.

To compromise, compromise, compromise—the whole strategy of the Enemy is to get us to compromise – to obey tomorrow instead of starting today, to pay eighty percent of the price instead of a hundred percent of the price. I beg you; straighten things in your life. Compromise! Compromise is a killer. You look at what God said and you look at what man said. You look at what God asked for and you look at what your own desires are.

Yesterday, when I was sharing with sister Emilia, repenting for accepting midnight as the time when some Nights of Prayer should start, in a new way I saw the tragedy of compromise. You heard the Lord clearly. You knew what you should do. The Enemy did not say, "No." He merely said, "Do it later."

"Give part of it. You will give the other part later on."

"You just need it. How can you do without it?" Compromise; O, compromise! O, the voice of the Enemy! The voice of the Enemy!

"O God, give me strength to be violently opposed to each suggestion. I've heard Your Voice. O God, the brethren have heard Your voice. Don't allow any to jump over what You have said because of comfort, because of ease, because of indulgence, because of uncertainty in the future, because of the apparent security that is offered. God, give each one of us the power to say; "No, no, no, no!—No, no, no, no" to Self, "no, no, no" to Self! "No, no, no" to that which has its origin in Self; no to that which looks innocent; "No" to that which looks harmless. It must be "Yes" to Your perfect will.

"Father, dismantle all compromised wills in the saints here. Father, use every instrument of heaven to block all that which is not the perfect will of God. Scatter! Scatter! Scatter! Scatter! Bring to nought! O Father, do it as an act of love. Oppose! Pull down! Puncture that which is not from You, that which is not Your perfect will. Father, what You allowed in Your permissive will, Father, we ask that You withdraw Your permissive will. Annul all such projects and annul all such projects and annul all such projects. Father, there shall be only one will – the perfect will of God! There shall be only one will – the perfect will of God! There shall be only one will – the perfect will of God! The perfect will of God! The perfect will of God! The perfect will of God!"

I call those husbands who allow things that they know are wrong, O, because their wives have resisted to repent. You will kill your wife! You will kill your wife! You will kill your wife! You may lose her forever. Say "No" and save her. You are the king! You are the prophet! You are the priest! Be unpopular with her so that she may live. Tear it down! Tear it down! Tear it down! If you don't have the courage, O lay hold on God! Lay hold on God! It might mean contradicting yourself. Contradict yourself a thousand and one times, provided you stay in the perfect will of God. You may be one man against a massive army of relatives and the like but God alone is with you. Victory is guaranteed. Take God's side! Take God's side! Take God's side! Take God's side over the Devil! The consequences of not taking God's side today and in the days ahead and in the weeks ahead–will cause you regret it if it were possible for millennia. Stop it! Stop it! Stop it! Stop it! Stop it! Stop it! Stop it!

To those of you who were at the Prayer Night and who prayed for me and set me apart to live out my Separation from the Common, as God called it, "The Blueprint for my Life, " – this separation does not allow me to have a jacket. In order that I may be true, I must take off this jacket. If you ever see me with a jacket, remove it and tear it up. I was told – four shirts, two pairs of trousers, two pairs of shoes, one suit. Forgive me for all the disobedience. I repent of the logic, the sin that beguiled me not to obey, the excuses that I am a travelling man.

Listen brother, the man of God who was sent to Jeroboam, was told, "Don't eat, don't drink, don't come by the same way" – very simple instructions. Great power was manifested as he ministered, but then, he yielded to a persuasive invitation, ate in disobedience and died. He was a disobedient prophet. There was an obedient lion. Disobedient prophets may have obedient lions to maul them.

Please, forgive me, forgive me. I abandon the reasons, I abandon the reasoning!

What qualified Joshua was the fact that he was Moses' servant. And he went up to the mountain top. If he went on his own, he would never be allowed to do so. But he went just as a servant, without a personal identity, and the Lord accepted him there. The Lord saw him, the Lord didn't mention his name. The Lord made as if he didn't see him. So Joshua now had the experience which, when the critical moment would come, he would be the only one who had seen the heavenly pattern of the tabernacle because as leader he had to be, in a sense, the custodian of the tabernacle. He had seen it as a Nobody and thus qualified to become God's custodian of the tabernacle. If he were not Moses' servant, he would not have gone, he would not have seen it.

Why was he chosen? He wanted all the glory and honour for Moses. He was not seeking for his glory. In Numbers 11, the Holy Spirit had come upon the people. Numbers 11 verse 25a,

> *Then the LORD came down in the cloud and spoke with him, and He took of the Spirit that was on him and put the Spirit on the seventy elders.*

The Lord could have put the Spirit directly on those people. He chose to take from Moses to the people so that there may be one Leader and one vision and one direction. Now they were mighty men. They were the 70 Elders. Yet God is bound by no rules. Two of the leaders were not there. Verses 26-27,

> *However, two men, whose names were Eldad and Medad, had remained in the camp. They were listed among the elders, but did not go out to the Tent. Yet the Spirit also rested on them, and they prophesied in the camp. A young man ran and told Moses, 'Eldad and Medad are prophesying in the camp.*

Joshua said, Verses 28b-29,

> *Moses, my lord, stop them! But Moses replied, 'Are you jealous for my sake? I wish that all the LORD's people were prophets and that the LORD would put His Spirit on them!*

Joshua was saying there should be only one leader – one Moses – the Spirit of God upon him, then the Spirit of the Lord from him to others. It was wrong reasoning but it was a correct heart. He was not dreaming about the day Moses would die and he would become the next leader. He was not dreaming about the day when he would be co-leader with Moses. There were no such thoughts. He saw Moses, Moses, Moses, Moses because he saw just God's purpose, God's purpose, God's purpose, God's purpose, God's purpose, God's purpose, God's purpose, God's purpose.

There were 200 other tribal heads but they rebelled. Joshua had might. Only great men can be loyal. Only great women can be loyal. Only people capable of doing their own things and doing them successfully can be loyal. He was a leader of his tribe. "From the tribe of Ephraim, Hoshea, son of Nun" – that's Joshua (Numbers 13:8). Where did "Joshua" come from? That was the name Moses had given to this Hoshea. He no longer bore his original name. When he became a servant, he took on the name his master had given him. A tribal leader – he had worked himself up through all that it takes to lead a tribe of Israel. He rose to the top. You see, he's the one who represented the tribe of Ephraim to go and spy out the Promised Land; mighty, the Number one man in Ephraim. Nonetheless, he became a servant.

He was a man of faith! He was a man of faith! When the twelve tribal leaders went and saw the Promised Land, he and Caleb brought back a report according to God. He was a man of faith and a man of vision. Faith and vision are indispensable for leadership. He saw what God saw, he believed what God believed and he proclaimed what God proclaimed! You know those twelve men, when they left to go and spy out the land, each one had written his report already because they went there and saw the same thing. So if they were reporting what they saw, they all would have brought the same report. But ten of these men did not believe what God had said. Caleb and Joshua believed what God had said. God had said that those tribes would be wiped out. God had said that the children of Israel would wipe out those tribes. That was on their hearts. So Joshua knew he was going to come back and say that these tribes would be dismantled according to what God had said. The other ten also had their reports. They went. People do not see with the eyes; they see with their hearts.

Say,

> *"I do not see with my eyes.*
> *I see with my heart.*
> *I do not see with my eyes.*
> *I see with my heart.*

> *I see according to what I have allowed God*
> *to print into my heart.*
> *I see according to what I have allowed God*
> *to infuse into my soul."*

Joshua and Caleb: Joshua was a man who could allow God to infuse into his heart what was in God's heart. Infuse! Infuse! Infuse!

Brother, I read the decision of faith by Martin Luther. It excited me. And John Wesley says as you go on with the Lord, if you walk in the holiness of God, in the perfection of God, the Holy Spirit infuses the attributes of God increasingly into you, infuses them into you so that you are transformed from one degree of glory to another.

Say,

> *"God,*
> *Infuse Your faith into my heart.*
> *I want to believe as You believe,*
> *And I want to believe what You believe.*
> *I want to believe as You believe*
> *And I want to believe as You, O my God,*
> *   believe.*
> *O God,*
> *Increase my faith here and now!*
> *O Lord,*
> *Increase my faith here and now!*
> *O Lord,*
> *Dismantle my unbelief here and now.*
> *O Lord,*
> *Dismantle my unbelief here and now –*
> *My unbelief of You,*
> *My unbelief of myself,*

> *My unbelief of my brother.*
> *O Lord,*
> *Do not only dismantle unbelief;*
> *Rend the heavens*
> *And pour faith into my spirit.*
> *Pour faith into my spirit –*
> *Faith in God,*
> *Faith in God.*
> *O God,*
> *Pour into my being*
> *Faith of the same kind as Your own.*
> *Lord, I believe that You have done it.*
> *I arise to a new level of faith tonight,*
> *I am able to do every good work.*
> *Amen!"*

He brought back a good report.

Have you met a son called Geuel?
Have you met someone called Geuel?
Have you met a Nahbi?
Have you met a Sethur?
Have you met an Ammiel?
Have you met Gaddi?
Have you met Gaddiel?
Have you met Palti?
Have you met Igal?
Have you met Shaphat? (Numbers 13:4-15)

No!

Who has met Calebs? Who has met Joshua? (Almost everybody) – Yes, those who bring good reports back. They continued. The others were destroyed.

I want to tell you, if you doubt God's testimony about you, it could be a sin unto death. If you doubt what God says about you, it could be a sin unto death. That's how Elijah died. God gave him all the promises, all the things he could do but he kept on saying, "O, I am not better than my fathers. I am not better than my fathers. All Israel has failed." When he said that again it was a sin unto death. God told him, "Do this, do this, do this." It is a dangerous thing when God says, "This is what you are," according to the heights of God and according to the knowledge of God, and you disbelieve Him because you don't want to look ahead; because you want comfort, you say, "I am not able." If you doubt what God has said about you – if God says, "I am giving you 10,000 people," and you say, "God, 500 are even many," you sin against Him. You know, one of the rare times that Moses annoyed God was when Moses was giving all the excuses, why he would not go and bring the people – "The Israelites will not believe me;" "I cannot speak." He was looking for reasons to spare himself from what God wanted him to do. And God was angry.

Exodus 4:10,

> *Moses said to the LORD, 'O Lord, I have never been eloquent, neither in the past nor since you have spoken to your servant. I am slow of speech and tongue.*

In Acts 7:22 it says,

> *Moses was educated in all the wisdom of the Egyptians and was powerful in speech and action.*

Moses who was mighty in speech and deeds now says, "I cannot speak," – trying to bury the talents and the gifts so that he would have an excuse to avoid the troubles of leadership. As a leader, your rest has ended. You do not know what the next telephone call will bring. Moses even denied the past. Like Peter, he said, "I don't know Him" and drew a curse upon himself. He said,

"O Lord, I have never been eloquent, neither in the past nor since you have spoken to your servant. I am slow of speech and tongue."

The LORD said to him, 'Who gave man his mouth? Who makes him deaf or mute? Who gives him sight or makes him blind? Is it not I, the Lord? Now go; I will help you speak and will teach you what to say (Exodus 4:10-12).

I will help you speak! I will help you speak! And I will teach you what to say! "I will help you speak and I will teach you what to say." – O, the promise of God! The promise of God! The promise of God! The promise of the living God! The promise of the living God! The promise of the living God! The promise of the living God! The promise of the living God! The promise of the living God! The pact of the living God! "I will help you to speak! I will teach you what to say.

Was Moses convinced? No.

Moses said,

O Lord, send someone else... (Verse 13).

The Bible says,

Then the Lord's anger burned against Moses (Verse 14a).

You have built your Ministry according to what faith you have in yourself. You have said, "Beyond this I cannot go." You said, "This is my quarter. By the time I die, I will plant 40 house churches here." OK, please add a zero. Add a zero. Add a zero to the 40.

Listen brethren, those of you who were in this hall when we came to break the first 40-day fast, in fact I had thought that that was the one last fast of my life, I had said I am not called to long fasts, so that I can help somebody along the fast and so, he will not say things that I don't know. The truth is that I don't have the gift of fasting. So when I have to fast for 56 days it is because I have no choice. One day the Lord told me, "All that you think, can be done because My greatness exceeds your highest thoughts." In that fast, sometimes it was so difficult to leave the room in Nkolbisson and come to the sitting room. But today—(stumping with all strength). That's why I am saying that you should rise and lay hold on God. Stretch, stretch, stretch, stretch and when you put down your foot, God will put down His own with you. Stretch out, stretch out!

Brother Constant phoned. We are arranging the trip to Sierra Leone because this weekend is Malabo, then Nigeria, then Togo, then Sierra Leone. This is the best time to go. First of all, I have to go to 50 nations this year. If I don't go fasting, I will not go.

What you proclaim, God will transform you into that. What you proclaim, God will transform you into that. O, I beg you, stand up and say something big. Stand up and lay hold on God for something big. Talk beyond your reasoning! Talk beyond your abilities!

"In the Name of Jesus Christ, I dismantle the chains with which you are bound. In the Name of Jesus Christ, I dismantle the chains with which you are bound. Let your hearts flow Godward. Let your hearts flow Godward."

The limits are set on earth; they are not set in heaven!

The limits are not set in heaven; they are set on earth!

"According to your faith, let it be done unto you!"

"I will do to you according to what I have heard your mouth say!"

Joshua was strong, able; he was the field marshal of the army. Joshua was the final authority in the Israeli army. And it's not weaklings that become that; the Number One soldier of Israel, mighty in deeds. God chose him because he was mighty. He had proved that he was mighty.

Listen, my brethren, are you striving to perfect what is already there? Are you striving to perfect what is already there? Are you faithful at what you are doing now, exceptionally faithful, so that God can now call you to do things that are exceptional? Are you pushing ahead so that God can now carry you to new heights?

Joshua – commander-in-chief; but he didn't plan his own wars. He had no wars. They were only God's wars and Moses' wars.

In Exodus 17:8-10a.

The Amalekites came and attacked the Israelites at Rephidim. Moses said to Joshua, 'Choose some of our men and go out to fight the Amalekites. Tomorrow I will stand on top of the hill with the staff of God in my hands. So Joshua fought the Amalekites as Moses had ordered.

Verse 13,

So Joshua overcame the Amalekite army with the sword.

Ah! Yeah! Yeah! Yeah! The victorious field marshal! The victorious field marshal! You know there were to be many wars on the other side of the Jordan. So he had what it would take to exercise leadership and he could follow.

Do you have the power to follow?

In one of the trips in Nigeria in those days when we just preached anywhere that doors were open in Nigeria, I went to one place I had been invited there by the students. I decided to go and visit the Vice Chancellor who was a believer. As we were chatting, I said, "There is a shortage of leaders in Africa." He told me, "I don't know; I think there is rather a shortage of followers." He was an older man. He was wiser. I was the young fool. Fools are always looking for leaders. It is the mark of a fool that he doesn't see the leader that is there. I was the fool. But I learnt a lesson that day. It will last all my life. It is easier to find a leader than to find a man who follows from the heart.

When I did this exercise, I named fifty leaders in our Ministry, people I can clearly see that they are leaders. I could not name five people who follow. To find a leader who follows —a man with leadership capacities, a man with obvious leadership capacities who follows from the heart, is a great miracle.

Joshua had might and the power to follow. There was a double anointing on him — the anointing to follow and the anointing for might. That's why God chose him. That's why God chose him. That's why God chose him.

Let me start at another angle. Is there a wife here who follows, who follows from the heart, who follows totally from the depth of the heart? I'm not asking who is struggling to ensure that her rebellion does not destroy everything, but who follows from the heart with joy, with gratitude.

Who here follows and God can say, "This one follows"?

Brethren, since we are preparing for the Season of Refreshing, since the Holy Spirit can only be poured on people whose hearts are fused together — one heart, one mind, one will - then perhaps the most obvious obstacle that is in the way is your inability to follow or the sins in following. Is that where you need to start now and ask the Holy Spirit to help you uproot all that must be uprooted? Can you pray for yourself just for a minute in this domain? Pray!

WHY GOD CHOOSES CERTAIN PEOPLE—GIDEON

Why did God choose Gideon to become a leader

Tuesday, 30th January, 2007.

Brethren. I want to say that about 75% of my time is spent thinking about leaders—how to produce leaders, I have spoken about leadership more than any other topic. In some countries they call me the Apostle of Prayer, but I've spoken more on leadership than on prayer. I've taught more on leadership than on prayer. So prayer is only secondary.

I asked God for leaders of five – a person who will lead five people; so that this person is known as a leader of five and he labours to become a leader of ten. I asked for some numbers:

leaders of 5.

Then leaders of 10,

Then leaders of 25,

Then leaders of 50,

Then leaders of 100,

Then leaders of 250,

Then leaders of 500,

Then leaders of 1,000.

A man who will say, "No, I am leading a thousand people," or "I lead 100 people; here they are," or "I lead 10 people."

I asked for leaders of 5,000,

I asked for leaders of 10,000,

I asked for leaders of 25,000,

I asked for leaders of 50,000,

I asked for leaders of 100,000,

I asked for leaders of 250,000,

I asked for leaders of 500,000,

I asked for leaders of 1 million,

I asked for leaders of 5 million,

I asked for leaders of 10 million,

I asked for leaders of 25 million,

I asked for leaders of 50 million,

I asked for leaders of 100 million.

I asked for leaders of 250 million,

I asked for leaders of 500 million,

I asked for leaders of 1 billion.

5	5,000	5,000,000
10	10,000	10,000,000
25	25,000	25,000,000
50	50,000	50,000,000
100	100,000	100,000,000
250	250,000	250,000,000
500	500,000	500,000,000
1,000	1,000,000	1,000,000,000

If we don't expand in leadership we cannot grow. A leader of 100 may have under him leaders of 10 and each leader of 10 has two leaders of 5:

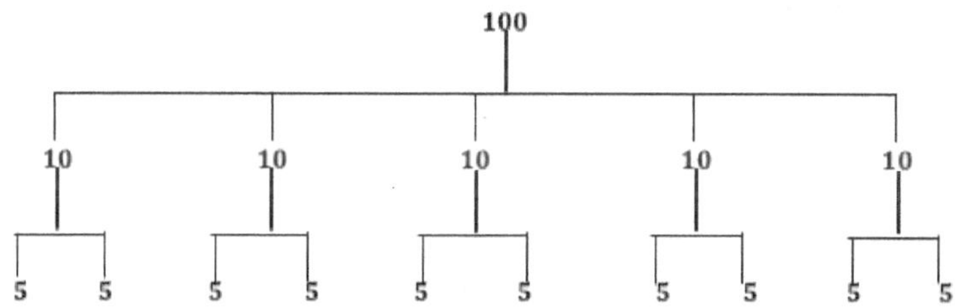

We must train leaders. We must train leaders. We must train leaders. But this is how I saw it in Douala and I was full of joy. Therefore a person will say, "I am a leader of 25. I am labouring to be a leader of 50." So his goal this year is to pass from a leader of 25 to a leader of 50. If he doubles, we have doubled. Then he begins to dream and plan for how he will become a leader of a hundred: How to produce leaders, How to produce the producers of leaders.

Brother J.M., I began to pray that God would urgently give us a place where we will meet once a month with a seating capacity of 25,000 in the city – because you must meet with all the people under you at least once a month, that's the minimum – just to tell them, "This is where we are going. This is where we are going. This is where we are going."

"Are we going up?"

"No, no, no, this is where we are going. This is where we are going. This is where we are going. This is where we are going."

And to those who have just believed, 'This is where we are going."

In fact, that's the work of the leader. Others can tell them but everybody must hear it from your lips once a month. The saying is, "From the horse's own mouth, from the horse's mouth."

Don't jump. If you are leading 10 people, just say, "God, make me a leader of 25" because when you start saying, "Make me a leader of 5000," you will be frustrated because it gives you a goal that you see but which you cannot work for its accomplishment at the moment.

Listen, already a family head is a leader of five, isn't he? His wife and four children or his wife and three or four other people living with them; he's a leader.

Pray that God would give everyone here the ambition to be a leader.

Lift up your hand and tell the Lord,

"I will be a leader and I will move from one level of leadership to another. Amen."

Why does God choose people to be leaders? Let's look at the case of Gideon. Why was Gideon chosen to be a Leader?

In Judges 6:14b,

Go in the strength you have and save Israel out of Midian's hand.
Am I not sending you?

He had strength. He had strength. Where did the strength come from?

In Verse 11,

The angel of the LORD came and sat down under the oak in Ophrah that belonged to Joash the Abiezrite, where his son Gideon was threshing wheat in a winepress to keep it from the Midianites.

He was working hard! Gideon was called to leadership from the place of working hard. He was working hard, working hard, working hard. He was putting all of his might to do what could be done in the circumstances. He was putting all of his physical force to do what he could do in the negative circumstances that prevailed. Strength, applied to work, in order to produce more strength.

Every book I've read on leadership—spiritual leadership and worldly leadership – and I've read not less than a hundred, you see everything hinges on hard work.

Look at Bill Clinton ... And brethren, let me tell you how I read the books. I read, first of all to find out what made him great. Then I read to find out what I can apply in my life. Bill Clinton was a workaholic. He slept very little, Sometimes even in class he would sleep for a minute. Sometimes the teacher would catch him. But it was such that one, two, three minutes of sleep could just renew him. He worked very, very hard. Brethren, when I finished reading the book, I was just amazed at what he accomplished. People don't know the story. This man did for America what has never come out anywhere else. We have a wicked world. Men pick out your fault and close their eyes to everything else that is good and say, "See, see." What this man did is enormous. And he started working at it from the age of 10. From the age of 10, he began to look at the Democratic Conventions on television. From the age of 10, he set out to be a politician. He had chosen one way. Listen, he was born after his father had died. There was no money, nothing, nothing, nothing. I think his mother married three times. Extreme hard work!

I've just finished reading another biography of John Wesley. It's the best of the eight that I've read because the man wrote to let us know why God used John Wesley. Brethren, I've read parts of it three, four times. And for those of you who have heavy feet, the book is 320 pages and it's the fourth book I've read for this year. Brethren, he worked; let me also tell you that he slept for six hours every night. He never missed one night of sleep for 50 years of life. He was reading on horseback and writing on horseback. I don't know how he was doing it. He rode 250.000 miles, (400,000 km) on horseback. He preached 800 sermons a year for 50 years – so maybe 40,000; 800 sermons a year on average for 50 years. He economised minutes as people would economise blood – hard work, hard work! Someone said, "Look at leaders. They may differ in what they believe and differ in their philosophy. They may differ in their attitude to human beings but all true leaders have one thing in common, they work exceptionally hard."

Paul says,

For I am the least of the apostles and do not even deserve to be called an apostle, because I persecuted the Church of God. But by the grace of God I am what I am, and His grace to me was not without effect. No, I worked harder than all of them - yet not I, but the grace that was with me (1 Corinthians 15.9-10).

Paul became the first of the apostles by working harder than them all. He did not talk about unusual power – but about unusual hard work. "I worked harder than them all, harder than them all, harder than them all" – therefore I came first of them all.

In 2Corinthians 11:23, when he talks about his marks of distinction, the first one is in verse 23, *I have worked much harder.* Then after that he talks about imprisonment and being beaten and the rest. "I have worked much harder."

Listen, my beloved; **you are where hard work has placed you**.

When we used to go to the farm, we started going before we were seven. I was born in June 1945. My elder sister was born in December 1941. We used to go to the farm together. Our parents used to send us together. Ma Hodia was still very young. When we got to the farm, l would tell my elder sister, "Just divide the area to be worked on into two" because I had noticed that when everybody was just working together, people would be working and relaxing. I said, "Just divide it." She was three-and-a-half years older but I always worked like mad – whether it was hoeing, whether it was weeding or whatever. I said, "Just divide it." I didn't understand how you could get to the farm and just be clearing and relaxing, clearing and relaxing. It was to finish in the shortest possible time and get away in the shortest possible time.

My advantage over many of you is that I work harder. I've read four books and one is 320 pages plus and I've read at least half of the book all over and I've made 24 pages of notes. Now, some of you have not finished your first book.

Pray that God would raise men and women of hard work in our midst because that's the determinant factor.

Listen brethren, I read in *Time Magazine* (it's a pity that I didn't photocopy it) about a leader of one of the communist countries of those days. For five years he never slept for more than two hours – working hard, working hard, working hard. When I read about Stalin, they would finish their meetings at 4 a.m. At 7 a.m. he would be back in the office.

R. B Woodworth, one of the best scientific brains of the last generation, would leave the laboratory at 4 a.m. At 7 a.m. he would return. This he did for over 40 years. It was said that when he saw someone going away at 1 a.m., he would look at him with a bad eye. He was awarded the Nobel Prize.

I did not read it, but brother Theodore A. told me that Margaret Thatcher worked twenty-one hours a day for about eleven years. She knew more than her ministers. She would read their documents more than them. So she would floor all of them.

Have you people read Kwame Nkrumah? He was up at 3:30 a.m. every day. Sometimes, just to shock his ministers, at 7 a.m. he would be phoning to see whether they were already in their offices.

In the annals of history, top leadership rests in the hands of those who work extremely hard.

My beloved, God is an Enemy of mediocrity. From different quarters, brethren said that I should write something about the author at the back page of the books. So one morning, I meditated on it. I began to write out what I could – things that would compel people to read me because if you are nobody, why should somebody bother to read you? A meeting I was to speak at in the U.S. was being advertised. The brother exaggerated the details ... I told him, "Brother, first of all repent. Do you need to say something about me for the meeting to hold?" He told me, "In Africa, people don't have use for their time. Here, people go to listen to those who have much to offer. There are so many speakers. If a man is going to sacrifice to come, something must convince him that this man has much to offer." In the next Meditation, I came back to the issue. That was four years ago. The Lord said, "Don't write anything behind the books until you have seven things in which you are more than a hundred." I didn't have then. Now I have twelve domains. I'll let you know.

- A hundred percent of all earned cash given to the Lord.
- A hundred percent of all cash gifts from every human being given to the Lord
- More than one hundred Christian books written i.e. by my editorial assistants and I.
- More than 50,000 written answers to Prayer.

Brethren, I have over 50,000 written answers to Prayer. They may be small Prayer Topics like, "Lord, let me have my Daily Dynamic Encounter today," but it was written and answered. There are over 50,000.

- I've read over 1200 Christian books.
- I've carried out more than 200 Fasts between 3 days and 52 days.
- I've carried out more than 600 Missionary journeys ranging from one day to twenty- one days in Cameroon.

There was a time I spent 21 days in Douala doing Church planting. We planted Churches in three quarters. We went to a quarter where there was no Church and held a seven-day

Campaign and then left a Church there. Of course, I was working with brother Martin F. and the leaders.

I've been out of Yaounde to preach the Gospel over 600 times. Sister Esther K. is my archivist. You see on her sheet (Prayer Bulletin for a trip) here, it's "Cameroon-Global." This Ministry in Mbalmayo will be the 635th time I've gone out of Yaounde to preach. And I've preached the Gospel in eighty localities in Cameroon; indicated at the top of this prayer sheet. When I will preach in another new area, it will be 81; but even if I go to that same place 50 times, it is just one town. It will be my third preaching in a town in Cameroon and my first trip to Mbalmayo this year. You have this other sheet – "Ministry in Jos". It will be the 444th time that I go out of Cameroon to preach the Gospel having preached in 58 nations. This will be the sixth nation in which I am preaching the Gospel this year. And it will be my first trip to the nation of Nigeria.

Brother, let me talk to you from my own heart. I don't have many abilities. When my results for the first degree came out and I won the University prize, Prof Owen (he was Head of Department) told me: "It's not a reward for unusual intelligence but it's a reward for unusual hard work." From Makerere University I got a letter last year. I obtained the PhD degree in the shortest time after the Bachelors degree. The record has not been beaten till today. That's what my bench mate wrote to me. I left the laboratory sometimes at 4 o'clock in the morning. I remember one day we were carrying out a chromatography of a compound that could rearrange on the column. And there was another isomer. So from the time I started to run the column I could not close the tap because it would lead to mixing of the isomers. Around 3:30 a.m., I was so tired – We carried the column and the receiver flask into the car and Prisca F. held it so that the column would keep running while I drove. I slept for one or two hours. At 7 o'clock in the morning she held the column while I drove back to the laboratory. Brother Joe B. was my classmate. My best position in class in Bali College ranged between third and seventh. I didn't work hard then. I owe it to my father who worked madly hard.

I want to tell you, everybody can work hard

- I've preached the Lord Jesus Christ in more than 200 localities on Planet Earth. In India alone I have preached in twenty-three localities.
- I have recorded more than 12,000 Dynamic Encounters with God.

And then I wrote 18 areas where I want to move ahead in order to bring them to a hundred. I read that 1% of leaders are born, 99% are made. So, brother, wherever you are, you can stand up and do great things. If I could beg you, please believe yourself and believe your God, and believe that you are able, and believe that it's not too late! At 80 years, Moses had nothing to show God. He started at 80, and there's no one like him. So don't say that it's late. It was not late for Moses at 80.

- In Chemistry, alone or with others, I have supervised a hundred dissertations from the Masters to the "Doctorat d'Etat." (PhD).
- I have more than 100 publications in International Journals.

I want to provoke the great people who are here. I want to provoke the great people who are here, I want to provoke the great person that you are to rise forth to your greatness, to rise forth to what you are, if even for no other reason, but for the very fact that God dwells in you, that Jesus Christ dwells in you, that the Holy Spirit dwells in you. O, brethren, can you take all that and just sit down and do nothing and frustrate God's urge to do great things through you? He came into you that He might do His great deeds in you and through you. He came into you so that the greatness of God might be exploded in you and exploded through you. When you place the limits, then you have placed the limits for God. If you move, God moves. If you don't move, God cannot move. Is it fair to reduce the God of heaven who dwells in you to a mediocrity? You are not only doing harm to yourself. You are doing harm to Him because He now looks like the God who fails, the God of mediocrity. Please, if only out of love for Him, give Him an opportunity to explode in you and explode through you.

Pray that the saints would receive from God the gift to believe themselves.

You see, brethren, you know many fasts that I broke after seven, eight, nine days; but I didn't say, "No, I cannot fast." There are no unscarred generals. Some of them have the scars of their failures. But they refused to settle in the face of their failure. I have been trying to do the fifty-two-day fast for over four years before I succeeded. You know last year I stopped one of the fasts on the eighteenth day, the other one after the twentieth day, but I gained something from it and I didn't give up the call to do ten supra-long fasts against the hosts of wickedness sin the heavenly places. If you fail, you have failed only for now. I don't know, but there's somebody, the first time he won the elections, he won as President of America. He had failed all the other elections. Who was that? – Abraham Lincoln. He won the election to become the Head of State.

Do you believe yourself? Do you believe the Triune God—Father, Son and Holy Spirit who dwell in you?

The verse that has become my verse for this year, since yesterday, let me tell you so that when you hear me praying, you don't say, "He has gone nuts!" This is my verse for the year.

It is John 14:11-14,

> *Believe me when I say that I am in the Father and the Father is in me; or at least believe on the evidence of the miracles themselves. I tell you the truth, anyone who has faith in me will do what I have been doing. He will do even greater things than these, because I am going to the Father. And I will do whatever you ask in my name, so that the Son may bring glory to the Father. You may ask me for anything in my name, and I will do it.*

Jesus presented miracles and asked that the people should believe at least because of the miracles. We shall present miracles in the largest numbers, miracles of the most peculiar kind so that those who want to believe because of miracles will believe then. The Lord says that he who believes in Him will do the things that He did. If you believe, you will do the things that He did but if you don't believe, I believe. I will do the things that He did. But that's not the end. The Lord has promised that we will do greater things than He did. Some people say, "No, I am not even doing what Jesus has done. How can I begin to talk about greater things?"

O.K., those who don't believe it, I will give you a pair of scissors to cut out that part of the Bible while saying, "This part is a lie."

O.K., you don't want to cut it out? O.K., you shall confess it. What is the condition? "He who believes in me."

Just read it aloud.

John 14:11-14,

> *Believe me when I say that I am in the Father and the Father is in me; or at least believe on the evidence of the miracles themselves. I tell you the truth, anyone who has faith in me will do what I have been doing. He will do even greater things than these, because I am going to the Father. And I will do whatever you ask in my name, so that the Son may bring glory to the Father. You may ask me for anything in my name, and I will do it.*

Pray that the brethren would receive the gift not only of believing God but of believing themselves.

The Lord said to Gideon,

> *Go in the strength you have and save Israel out of Midian's hand* (Judges 6:14b).

Go in this strength that you have. Gideon complained, "How can I save Israel?"

> *But Lord,' Gideon asked, 'how can I save Israel? My clan is the weakest in Manasseh, and I am the least in my family'* (Judges 6:15a).

But he had what was needed – the power to work hard, a hardworking Gideon and God as his partners would grant him success.

Verse 16,

> *The Lord answered, I will be with you, and you will strike down all the Midianites together.*

Recruiting a hardworking man to team up with the Almighty God produced a victorious team! In this matter of hard work, indulgence is an enemy. Gideon's original army was 32,000 strong. It was reduced to 10,000 after the test of fear to go to war. Those who were prepared to go home, who had a justifiable reason for going home, were allowed to return. Only those who were determined to war were allowed. This willingness to strike, this willingness to fight, this willingness to conquer – that's what many brethren don't have or they don't want. They look for excuses.

By the grace of God, by the time I finish the fast on the 4th of March, I will have gone to eight countries and to five localities in Cameroon outside Yaounde. Brethren, I could also have settled and said I am fasting. The limits are not set in heaven, they are set on earth. If you say that, "I will just lie in my bed and turn about because I am fasting," you will lie down and turn about because you are fasting. If you say, "I am fasting; I cannot have Meditations, so will it be. If you decide to tap the power that is released in fasting in order to do what you could not do when you were not fasting, it will also be so. The willingness to strike! The willingness to strike! The willingness to strike! When you say, "I am tired," OK, you are tired. When you say, "I cannot do it," OK, it will not happen. But if you say, "I will do," you will do it. If you say, "Fasting is not a disease; it is a feast, a feast of rejoicing," then you will be rejoicing. If you say, "Oh, it's a time of misery; Oh! Oh! Oh! Oh. If you say, "It's a feast of rejoicing, a feast of rejoicing" and that you will celebrate, your body will take up with you to give you a celebrating body. It will take up your confession to give you a celebrating body. "God will do to you according to what He has heard you say. You say. "Here is the limit," God agrees and says, "OK." If you say, "There lies the limit," God will say, "OK." If you say, "The limit is the sky," so will it be. Say, "God has given me the power to set the limits." Say it!

"God has given me the power to set the limits."

Look at this man, John Wesley, who has shaken the world – There are about 15 million Methodists in the world today. Do you know how tall he was? – Five feet (1 metre 50), five feet. He could have said, "Weeh, God, why did You make me short?" He has done what people who were perhaps two metres tall did not do. His parents were poor. His father went to prison for four months because he couldn't feed his family. He borrowed money to feed his family and so went to prison for four months. He was a Pastor. He just baptised someone when he was arrested and locked up for four months. He didn't complain that he came from a poor family. His mother said, "It's one of the sad things in this family that your father and I never see the same on any issue." He didn't say, "O my parents, it has not worked." He got an engagement when he was in America and it led to trouble. He even fled from America to run away from the problems that were coming up. In another instance when he wanted to get married to some woman, the brethren, especially his brother, helped the woman to marry another person before he arrived. Then he saw this other woman and just married her before he disclosed it to people. And the marriage was a fiasco. He didn't say, "My marriage is bad. I am done for." He went on and, and on, and on, and on, and on, and on, and on, and on. There are more books written on John Wesley than any other person in living history. As the father of a denomination, he has the largest number that came from one person's ministry as the starting point. I am just talking about what could have made him give up – his own stupidity, yes, his own stupidity. Nevertheless, he went ahead and triumphed!

Do you have the will to strike? Do you have the will to strike? Is your gaze fixed ahead or are your eyes are fixed on your past failures?

Someone told me, "I can't understand: you say you are going to fast for twenty-one days; you stop on the tenth day and just the next moment you are rejoicing and planning the next thing." Brethren, I decided that the Devil will not have two victories. If he prevents me from accomplishing what I should accomplish, that's his only victory. After all, I have only failed that time: I have not failed forever. Why do you make one instance an eternal issue?

The will to strike! Stretch out your hand and try the first time. Stretch out your hand and try the first time to strike.

Twenty-two thousand people would not even attempt to go to war. These were chosen soldiers, able men, yet twenty-two thousand lacked the courage to strike. This is the most powerful weapon of Satan – the multitude of people who don't act.

Pray that God would transform the ten thousand that we are in the city, each one of us into a striking element for God's victory in the city.

Dare to believe God! Dare to believe yourself! Dare to believe yourself! Dare to believe yourself! Forget the failures of the past! Dare to believe that God has not given you up. Have faith to believe that God has not given you up to lower plans. That He has not buried the best He had and has the leftovers.

Listen, the prodigal son smashed everything when he went astray. However, he came home to a promotion. Before he went away, the best garment was not put on him. No ring was on his finger. He had been offered neither special shoes nor a fatted calf. God always restores with a promotion! God always restores with a promotion! If you failed here (at first level), God does not restore you at same level. He restores you with a promotion! He restores you with promotions! He restores you with promotions! He restores you with promotions! The prodigal son was asking that he be restored with demotions. That was the best he could think of. God, the Father, did not restore him to where he was! He restored him to a higher place! He restored him to a higher place! He restored him to a higher place! He restored him to a higher place! He restored him to a higher place! He restored him! He used to eat before he went. Now he was feted, he was feted. Lift up your eyes! Lift up your eyes and look at the great plans that God has for you! That is the minimum to which you will be restored. All the failures of the past buried in the love and forgiveness of our God! O, the God that restores with promotions! He had a promotion with regards to what he wore. He had a promotion with regards to the ring, promotion with regards to the shoes, and promotion with regards to the food, then with regards to the feast – five domains of promotion! One failure, and then you are welcomed with five promotions!

I read one author; it's in the book, *Charles Cowman*. She said, "If America did not exist, God would have had to create another new world for Christopher Columbus to discover. Because of what he put in, he had to discover a new world. She said, "If America did not exist, God would create another new world."

Why did God choose and use Gideon? We have seen that twenty-two thousand men disqualified themselves because they lacked the willingness to strike. This is a serious matter, brethren.

Some of you don't give to World Conquest. You have money but you just lack the will to give. I want five thousand gifts from the Church in Yaounde this month. Send me a note with it, "Brother Zach, take these 5 francs as a contribution to ensure that the nation and the nations are taken for God." No, one franc – from one franc to any amount. We now have a one franc coin. I want ten thousand such gifts. Get your children, even the sucklings to send their envelopes. Brethren, for the first time, my hands are tied since we started the Ministry. I cannot obey clear instructions from God. Get everybody in your house, each one with his own envelope, from one franc to any amount, between now and the end of February. Put your name there or if it is your baby, put its name – Just the will to act.

Gideon now had ten thousand people. They had to pass the final test. The Lord said,

> *There are still too many men. Take them down to the water, and I will sift them for you there. If I say, 'This one shall go with you,' he shall go; but if I say, 'This one shall not go with you,' he shall not go* (Judges 7:4b).

Soldiers are appointed by the Lord. These ones had chosen to fight. These ones had said they will fight.

Some years ago, I bought an old *Volkswagen* car, It was a silly act. It broke down on the way from the city centre to the National Assembly building. I was there cleaning the spark plugs and fidgeting with other things. Brother Peter Schneider said to me, "This is a joke" – that I should be driving a car that could break down in town, a joke that I should be cleaning spark plugs and removing dead parts. That was the folly of those days.

If I go to brother Joe Gado's house and I see him washing plates or cooking and he claims it is humility, I will call it the highest arrogance because there are things that only he can do. And while he's doing what others can do, those things that only he can do will suffer. It will not be humility; it will be great arrogance. His action says, there's nobody who can wash plates; there is no one who can cook. I'm the only one who can." It's great arrogance. I'm talking to all of us.

We said comfort and compromise lead to mediocrity. You can replace comfort with indulgence.

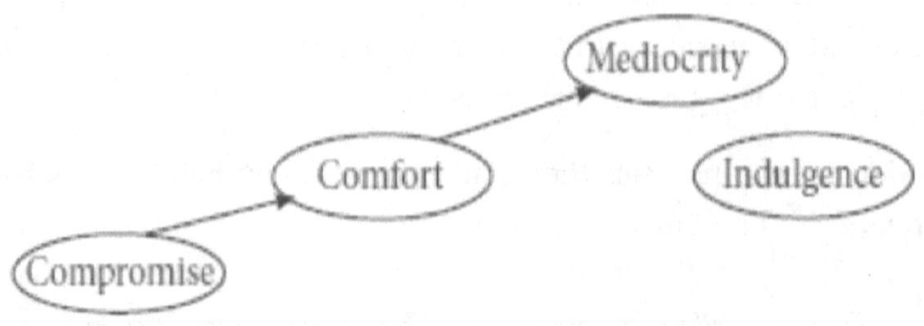

Brother, there are possibilities of sacrificing much on the altar of comfort, on the altar of indulgence. Small things expose the depths of the heart. The overcomers were separated from the others just by the way they drank water. It looked like a small matter but it exposed the heart. "Separate those who lap the water with their tongue like a dog from those who kneel to drink." They really went for the comfort of drinking. They knelt so that from a position of comfort they would really drink. That's indulgence. That's how the heart was known. They wanted the comfort of drinking. The other ones who lapped just wanted water to keep their system going. And those who wanted the comfort of drinking — indulgence, indulgence, comfort; indulgence, comfort; indulgence, comfort; indulgence, comfort, indulgence - were eliminated.

O my beloved, is that the altar on which you have sacrificed everything? – Comfort. "I want to be comfortable. I want to be comfortable. I want ease." It leads only to mediocrity. What are you compromising in order to be comfortable? Compromising in order to be comfortable? Compromise, comfort, indulgence is burial of leadership. Only 300 out of 32,000 – God wanted 32,000 leaders but only 300 were offered to Him. Who eliminated them? – They themselves. In fact, only you can eliminate yourself. Only you can eliminate yourself. Only you can eliminate yourself. If you compromise, if you indulge, if you choose comfort, you will end up a mediocrity. We saw that Gideon was chosen because he worked hard. As the battle went on, in Judges 8:4, it says, *Gideon and his three hundred men, exhausted yet keeping up the pursuit, came to the Jordan and crossed it.*

O faint but pursuing! Faint but pursuing! Faint but pursuing! Faint but pursuing! Faint but pursuing! Faint but pursuing! Faint but pursuing! Faint but pursuing!

O brethren, and that's again the grave of so many. When they are tired, they withdraw. When they are tired, they withdraw. That's laziness! That's laziness! That's laziness!

There will be times when the leader will have to lead for twenty-four hours non-stop. There will be times when he will lead for forty-eight hours non-stop. There will be times when he will lead for seventy-two hours non-stop. There will be times when he may have to lead for seven days non-stop. Now, if he's a man who works hard, then goes and rests, works hard, goes and rests, he can no longer lead the troop in a crisis when it will be a make or break necessity that he stays at the battlefront. The habit of a lifetime of hard work, rest, hard work, rest, hard work, rest will eliminate him. Faint but pursuing! Faint but pursuing! At the end of his energies yet he continues so that God has to impart energy to him supernaturally. Many brethren do not know the special interventions of God because they do not get to the total end of themselves so that God is compelled to act.

Brethren, last year I worked as I had never worked in my life. From October it was as if any moment I could collapse. Were it not for the certainty that if I collapse, I would collapse into His arms, I would not have continued. I was rich in my spirit but physically and emotionally.... I travelled to 35 nations, some of them three times. I went to 26 different localities in Cameroon, some places three, four times. And, of course, when you visit, you are drained to the finish.

I want to say, brother, below are the arms of God. Even if you collapse, you will collapse into His arms. If you decide to stretch the limit to which you can go, keep stretching the limit to which you can go, you will gain new grounds, you will go further, further, further and further.

This year we will go to fifty nations because, as never before, I am, seeing the harm of not visiting the nations, visiting the brethren, and the blessings of visiting them. If I had said, "OK, I will go to thirty-six nations," then I have decided to frustrate the stretching out principle.

John Wesley said, "Either you are moving ahead or you are backsliding." Anything you have that you do not add to, there is decline. If this year you decide to give God the same percentage as you did last year, you have decided to backslide. The only way not to backslide is to keep moving ahead! The only way not to backslide is to keep moving ahead! Last year I had 400 Meditations. This year, the goal is 500. You cannot repeat and not backslide. Success is always pressing into new areas! Always pressing into new areas! Always pressing into new areas! If you stand still, you must go back.

The person who is not forging ahead is being pushed backwards.

We refuse to listen to the language of the body! We refuse to listen to the language of the body! In the past, if I had problems in my stomach or a fever while fasting, I would stop the fast. That was foolishness and ignorance. I've taken malaria medication four times since the fast started. If i wanted a good reason to stop the Fast, I would have had it. But woe is me if I stop because of the hosts of wickedness in heavenly places that must be dismantled.

Brethren, it is sad to see the small excuses, the small obstacles that cause people to give up very great projects, that cause people to give up very great results. Just a small obstacle, a flimsy thing, and great things are given up. Just pain for a moment, just tiredness for a moment, just a painful word from somebody, and great dreams, great visions, great possibilities are abandoned. That's why, my beloved, you need someone to whom you have given the final rights in your life, to whom you have said, "When in my folly I want to draw back, fight with me; don't let me have my way." In the accomplishment of great projects, there comes a moment when a person feels like giving up, to compromise, to settle on the wrong side of the Jordan. He needs someone to whom he had previously handed his life without reservations to tell him, "No, you will not stop:" to tell him, "If you die, die. I will take the responsibility but you will continue."

Who is that person in your life? – Because in those delicate moments if there was just some support lasting five minutes, or one hour, you will recover the spirit of fighting and the story will be different. And that's what life is about.

In my battles to give to God, there was one delicate battle. But for Henriette K., I would have conceded defeat. Then I gained strength and didn't need any encouragement after that. And if I had compromised then I would have just kept going down. When you start giving according to logic with regards to your salary you are still a poor man; no question about it. Anybody who gives knows that with his whole salary intact, he is still a poor man. His needs are more than that salary. So when you start going down, you see your needs more clearly and reduce the percentage more until you say, "God even understands the fact that I will give next year." O, you need somebody! You need somebody! You need somebody! You need somebody who keeps his head when you are losing yours, to hold your hand maybe for a minute or ten minutes or one hour and then you recover the balance and then you keep going. But the authority to so act has to have been conferred to the person in normal times. Then he can use the authority during the crisis.

Pray that this would be seen.

Both by what the Lord said to me personally and by what I said to Him and by what I saw in the Bible, it is not possible to vow and not fulfil the vow and remain the same. God will destroy the works of your hand. A vow in the Old Covenant was binding. In the New Covenant the word of a believer has the power of an Old Testament vow and more. If people could not run away from their vows in the Old Testament and remain the same, then in the New Covenant a believer cannot walk away from his promises and remain the same.

I put together what God asked of me and what I promised God. As I've studied the Scriptures more and more, and at the calling of God. I must keep my vows! I must live out my Separation from the Common. I've gathered it in bits slowly over the years. The document was offered to God as a vow. I need help. Help me to live it out, to begin to live it out totally.

I'm like a man who was in a canoe in a stream in control of everything. I've just entered into a massive river! I'm shaken in all directions. Pray with me that I would take my balance and just obey all that God asked me and all that I promised Him. It's the fiercest conflict of my life. I've battled with it on all planes – how it will affect my relationships, how it will affect my generosity, and so on and so forth. That's logic. I just have to obey. Let me mention three things that affect you.

- I cannot embrace you anymore. I said it; it must be.
- I cannot receive gifts from you except food, hospitality and transportation.
- Thirdly, if you want to say something negative about somebody to me, you must bring along the person; if you do not, don't say it.

The inner requirements:

- I must never think any negative thought about anyone regardless of what he's done to me or to us.
- I must never wish anyone anything less than God's best.
- I must never ask God to judge anybody.
- I must never sin in my heart.
- I must never think or do anything that cannot be exposed, written across the skies.
- I must never hold back anything from anyone who asks me.
- I must never keep anything that I don't need immediately while someone is in need and asks me for it.
- I must never say I am tired.
- I must never say I have no money.

- I must never stop a fast before the day I am asked to stop it.
- From now on I'm not allowed to do any fast that is less than fifty days because even after the ten fasts against the hosts of wickedness in the heavenly places, there are other satanic forces to be confronted – the Rosicrucian Order, the Freemasons and numerous hosts of wickedness still in the heavenly places.

Pray for me. I was commanded to get this written as a book and circulate it. I've told the Lord over a thousand times and I've given all the reasons why it should not be done. But when you have been told the same thing seven times, you obey or perish. It's as if I've tied myself—mouth, nose, every part of me is tied. Just to help you understand, three times I've tried to raise a dead man to life and failed. The Lord said the power to raise the dead is the final anointing which was not given in the Bible to many, and that there are very harsh prices to pay to attain it. Pray for me that I may settle in my Separation from the Common because that's the condition for raising the dead so that if someone died in our midst or I were called to raise the dead somewhere, I would not fail again because the raising of the dead is part of the ministry of the New Covenant.

When I see our sister Lydienne M. in a wheelchair, when I see Aggie T. without sight, that's not God's perfect will. God's total will is that each one should be in perfect health from conversion to rapture. We have healings all over but the number who are not healed tells me this is not it, because nobody ever came to the Lord Jesus Christ and returned with his disease; not one. I believe we will get there. When I think about the Fosso children, we are seeing only a part of what we should see. Since my Separation from the Common is like the locks on my head, I establish them so that the Enemy might be impotent and have no grounds to resist.

I used to chew "bitter kola" during fasts and I recommend it to you strongly because it's a mild laxative. Even on the thirty-third day you may pass faeces and be spared the agony on the last day of the fast where you sit on the toilet in pain as the pain forces you to alternate sitting on each buttock to ease the stool out and relieve you of the discomfort. Whenever I thought about the end of the fast it was the going to the toilet that was a nightmare. You know it, brother; you know it. Some of you have experienced it. The "bitter kola" will ease the faeces out slowly without any discomfort and your stomach will not suffer from shock. You can break the fast without going through all the discomfort. In fact, when we write the next book, *Practical Helps for Fasting Believers*, I will mention it there just as we have said about calcium. Dr. Ngufor G. had to break the faeces from somebody's anus. He had to wear gloves and begin to manipulate to break it. We want to stop that. If you take one in the morning and one in the evening, you will have no problem; fasting is not meant to look for problems. The challenge at the end of the fast is not that you cannot sit down on the toilet seat. The Lord said to me, "Don't[1], because if you do, the Devil will resist you." I am in conflict with the Devil at levels where the Lord sees that doing so will give him grounds to resist. That peculiarity is mine and His call on my life.

Now, writing to all our children that they should not send me gifts, a letter which I will write tonight, is putting a knife into my whole being; the pain it will cause them, and my lovers and my friends ... . But it has to be. Let it be so, so that what the Lord promised, because the Lord said that the dead will be brought here and raised here in Obili and the Lord said that at Obili people will tell us, "Someone is dead here," and we will pray from here and the person will be raised to life thousands of miles away. Let me pay the price so that when those days come we shall not be impotent.

Let me say, brother, we are not competing with each other; we are complementing each other We are not competing with each other rather, we are complementing each other. Today in my office, I was reading a message that the Lord gave about my Ministry and brother Joe M.'s Ministry. We are complementing each other, therefore we are given different gifts as our tools for complementation, and asked to do different things as a means of advancing our complementarity. I insist! We are not competing with each other; we are complementing each other. This applies not only to him but also to each one of you. We complement each other. We are in a massive Ministry. Bring along the contribution that you can bring in. You don't need the contribution that another person should bring. Bring along what you must bring in. Bring along all you must bring in! If you are the eye, see. If you are the nose, smell. If you are the ear, hear. And then we will give God what He wants. The Lord Jesus Christ will have all the glory.

WHY GOD CHOOSES CERTAIN PEOPLE—JEPHTHAH

Why God chooses some people; Why did God choose Jephthah?

Tuesday, 6th February, 2007.

Why does God choose some people?

The Word is received to be translated into action. Until you have translated what you hear into acts, you've not done anything. What have you done with what you have heard on spiritual leadership?

Please, reserve some part of your notebook where you write what you will act on.

Why did God use Jephthah?

Listen, his mother was a prostitute.

Judges 11:1b. *His father was Gilead; his mother was a prostitute.*

What a liability to have a prostitute for a mother. But we want to say there is hope. We want to say there is hope. Even if your mother was a prostitute or your father a prostitute or your father a murderer, whatever their crime, whatever their evil, great things can happen to you. Jephthah was driven away. Your past may be very terrible – driven away, unwanted. Yet he became the leader.

Say,

> *Regardless of my background,*
> *Regardless of the tragic condition of my*
>   *parents,*
> *Regardless of their horrible sins,*
> *I can still rise to God's heights.*

What did God see in Jephthah that made Him choose Jephthah? It was not just the fact that he could fight. God saw in Jephthah a man who feared God, a man who feared God, a man who feared God, a man who trembled before God's Word. God saw in Jephthah a man who was prepared to ruin his all in order to please God. Jephthah had depths, breadths and heights. Jephthah was a man who said, "I prefer to come to nought than to displease God."

We have been thinking about writing a book on the fear of God. As I was preparing this message, it dawned on me that there were few people in the Scriptures who feared God like Jephthah. When Jephthah was going to war he made a vow to the Lord, Judges 11:30-31,

> *And Jephthah made a vow to the LORD: "If you give the Ammonites into my hands, whatever comes out of the door of my house to meet me when I return in triumph from the Ammonites will be the LORD's, and I will sacrifice it as a burnt offering."*

The Holy Spirit was upon him when he made this vow because verse 29a reads,

Then the Spirit of the LORD came upon Jephthah.

The word came out of his mouth. The word came out of his mouth.

Verses 32-33,

Then Jephthah went over to fight the Ammonites, and the LORD gave them into his hands. He devastated twenty towns from Aroer to the vicinity of Minnith, as far as Abel Karamim. Thus Israel subdued Ammon.

God enabled him to crush the enemy and return home in triumph. Verse 34-35,

When Jephthah returned to his home in Mizpah, who should come out to meet him but his daughter, dancing to the sound of tambourines! She was an only child. Except for her, he had neither son nor daughter. When he saw her, he tore his clothes and cried, 'Oh! My daughter! You have made me miserable and wretched, because I have made a vow to the LORD that I cannot break.'

His only daughter had to be sacrificed as a burnt offering because he had spoken. Words had come out of his mouth and there was no way he could withdraw them. That's integrity. It is matching deeds with words. What is integrity? It is matching words with deeds. Integrity is matching words with deeds. Words have gone up like this; deeds must follow:

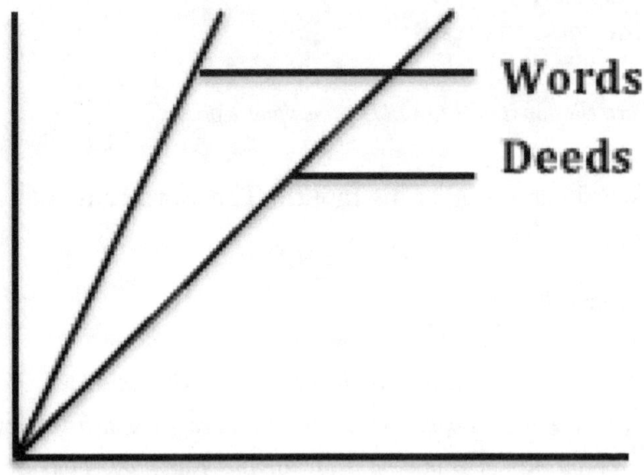

Matching words with deeds, that is integrity – at any price, at all cost. That's the fear of God. That's the character of the man! That's the character of the man! That's the character of the man! That's the character of the man! That's the character of the man! When God saw it, He chose him and empowered him to go and win and to lead His people. Matching words with deeds! Matching words with deeds! "I've given my word to the Lord! I've given my word to the Lord! I've given my word to the Lord! I've given my word to the Lord!" He didn't say, "O, I didn't know that it will be my daughter. No, God, You know I have got only one child. Please understand."

Crumbling minds, crumbling personalities, crumbling consciences expect God to understand! It is evil beyond telling! Evil beyond telling! Evil beyond telling!

"I've made a vow to the Lord that I cannot break."

To keep his vow he would be childless all his life. And that's what he chose rather than to be untrue to God, rather than say, "God, allow me to change my mind." When words have gone up to God, Oh, they cannot be withdrawn! They cannot be withdrawn, Deeds must back them. Deeds must back the words! Deeds must back the words! If not, you have a crumbling man with a crumbling conscience, with a crumbling personality.

Oh, and the man had a daughter of the same kind. If you see a crook, the daughter will be a crook. Don't look at the mother to know what the daughter will be like. Look for the father.

"Na wetin Papa dey do Oh, Oh, girlie go do am Oh! Oh! Oh! Oh!" What a father does, the daughter will do likewise.

It is the daughters that personify the father. When you marry the daughter of a corrupt man, you have decided to weld yourself to corruption. The daughter will not be like the mother. First of all, they spend all their time fighting with their mothers. Go and look for the father. She's the father in a gown. Please, I've studied this. I've studied this extensively. When you see the character of the father, you will see it in the daughter. You can ignore the character of the mother but you will see the father in the daughter. Who agrees? - Not just by sentiment. I'm telling you what people have researched and researched and researched. So when you see a corrupt man, flee from the daughter! If you see a man of virtue, go for the daughter! "I have made a vow to the Lord that I cannot break." This bonding between daughter and father, this reproduction of the character of the man in the daughter, she may physically look like the mother but she has the character of the father.

Verse 36,

> *My father, she replied, "you have given your word to the LORD. Do to me just as you promised, now that the LORD has avenged you of your enemies, the Ammonites."*

She did not say "Oh, Papa, can you not ask God to change His mind? Can you not withdraw your word?" Her father knew that what he said was irrevocable. His daughter knew she had to die. She only asked for two months before she died. After that she came and yielded herself to death so that the man's word to God might not fall to the ground.

This morning, at the command of the Lord, I gave my "Separation from the Common" to be published, to put chains to the vows I made to God and to His commands to me so that my heart that wants freedom may settle along the lines of the collar that I put on my neck, the chains that I put around my wrists and my ankles to walk under sealed orders.

Verse 39 says,

> *After the two months, she returned to her father and he did to her as he had vowed. And she was a virgin.*

The Bible says in Psalm 15:1,

> *LORD, who may dwell in Your sanctuary? Who may live on Your holy hill.*

Among a number of things it says, ...*who keeps his oath even when it hurts* (Psalm 15:4b).

What is binding on me hurts deeply. It shatters my heart. But I have no choice. Ecclesiastes 5 verses 4-6 say,

> *When you make a vow to God, do not delay in fulfilling it. He has no pleasure in fools; fulfil your vow. It is better not to vow than to make a vow and not fulfil it. Do not let your mouth lead you into sin. And do not protest to the temple messenger, 'My vow was a*

mistake.' Why should God be angry at what you say and destroy the work of your hands?

If I don't keep my vows I give the works of my hands to God for destruction. One more verse – I was shocked when I saw it.

Zechariah 5:3-4,

And he said to me, 'This is the curse that is going out over the whole land; for according to what it says on one side, every thief will be banished, and according to what it says on the other, everyone who swears falsely will be banished.' The LORD Almighty declares, 'I will send it out, and it will enter the house of the thief and the house of him who swears falsely by my name. It will remain in his house and destroy it, both its timbers and its stones.'

I could abandon my vows. I could abandon what I've said to God that I will be and I will do but I would have installed a curse of perjury that will eat and destroy me, destroy my family, destroy my progeny. At all cost, I must keep my vows and all of them are applicable now and there is no return. Also, if I tell God, "I've changed my mind, let's cancel it" and He says, "OK, My son, I've changed my mind. The covenant to save you no longer applies." "A man who swears to his own hurt; he keeps to his vow even when it hurts." It comes back to what we've said: Self-sacrifice or self-denial leading to suffering and then to greatness; or compromise leading to comfort, leading to mediocrity.

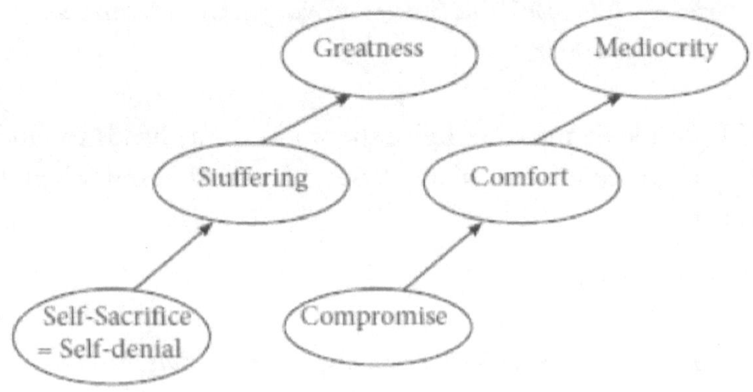

If you keep your promise to God, you will suffer but it will lead to greatness. But you can compromise it, push it aside. You will not suffer but you will be a mediocrity. It is easy to convince yourself to forget—forget what you said, forget what you promised – forget and go on. But you will end up as a mediocrity; your children, mediocrities; your grandchildren, mediocrities.

I beg you to pray for me. Nothing has ever hurt so deeply. Nothing will be so effective. It's as if I've signed away all my pleasure. But I will win a crown. I will lay it at His feet. We will win a crown, many crowns. We will lay them at His feet.

WHY GOD CHOOSES CERTAIN PEOPLE–SAMSON

Why God chose Samson to lead

Tuesday, 20th February, 2007.

Why did God use Samson? Samson was separated from the common. But I want to take one step back. When you see a great man or a great woman, take one step back. You may sometimes have to take two steps back.

God has given me unusual capacities to handle finances and unusual capacity to make money. To have given God 59 million 600 thousand francs (59,600,000 CFA francs) last year in our circumstances required the most unusual to take place. And to have given Him 61 million the year before, where was this money from? – My father, my father – when he left school, he was given a job on 18 pence a month in the local administration. A Missionary said to him, "Come and preach the Gospel. I'll give you 3 pence every 3 months" –

that means one penny a month. And by a miracle of God, by a miracle of God, by a miracle of God, he rejected this (18 pence salary) and accepted the one penny job. It was a separation from the common, a separation from logic. That's why you also stand to lay a foundation for your children. My father laid a foundation—by logic, absolutely foolish choice – no prestige, village preacher instead of being what they called the Court Clerk for the whole tribe of 26 villages. It takes an act of God for a man to make such a choice. The foundations that are laid for the future are foundations that are laid by acts of faith - seeing by revelation. This day I was weeping and sealing my Separation from the Common. I will never own property on earth. I had thought that I would get a large piece of land for my family in Bertoua. It will not be anymore. I will own no square metre on earth. The Etoug Ebe house will be sold immediately we leave for Bertoua and the money invested in heaven. As we said at the Prayer Night today, we must provide the foundations on which the blessings and the favours of God will fall. They cannot fall in the air. It is a man to provide the foundation on which the blessings of God will fall so that skyscrapers are built for God. If there are no foundations, the blessings will not fall because God will not let them fall to the ground.

Coming back to Samson, Judges 13:2-4,

> *A certain man of Zorah, named Manoah, from the clan of the Danites, had a wife who was sterile and remained childless. The angel of the LORD appeared to her and said, "You are sterile and childless, but you are going to conceive and have a son. Now see to it that you drink no wine or other fermented drink and that you do not eat anything unclean.*

She was separated from the common because others could drink wine, others could drink fermented drink, but she was not allowed to, Verse 5a,

Because you will conceive and give birth to a son.

"Because you are to give birth to this son who will be of special use to God, you cannot live like other women." It was like chains were placed on her. I've asked myself why they did not place any chains on the man. The child was to be in the woman's womb – But the woman had a more intimate relationship with God than the man. God puts chains not on everybody but on those who beg for chains to be put around their wrists, on their ankles.

About Samson,

No razor must be put on his head because the boy is to be a Nazirite, set apart unto God from birth, and he will begin to deliver the children of Israel from the hands of the Philistines.

Set apart unto God! Set apart unto God! Set apart unto God! Set apart unto God! Set apart unto God! Set apart unto God! Set apart unto God! Set apart unto God! Loss of freedom! Loss of freedom! Loss of freedom! Set apart unto God! The higher you go, the more loss of freedom.

When you choose to be free, to do what you want, where you want, with whom you want, you will be at the lowest rungs. If you are going to be at the top, a collar will be put on your neck, chains will be put on your feet and chains will be put on your wrists deliberately.

Of Joseph it was said, Psalm 105:16-22,

He called down famine on the land and destroyed all their supplies of food;

And He sent a man before them - Joseph, sold as a slave.

They bruised his feet with shackles, his neck was put in irons,

till what he foretold came to pass, till the word of the LORD proved him true.

The king sent and released him, the ruler of the peoples set him free.

He made him master of his household, ruler over all he possessed,

to instruct his princes as he pleased and teach his elders wisdom.

He had no freedom, It is a law of the spiritual life; it's also a law even in the natural world. When Jesus Christ came as King, where was He born? – In the place of absolute poverty. Where did He lie? – In the place of absolute poverty. He had no place to lay His head. He had only one set of clothes. One morning, coming out of Bethany, He was so hungry early in the morning that He went to look for fruit on a fig tree that was not in fruiting season. The disciples were not hungry so they had eaten. He had not eaten. If somebody thinks that the leader should possess more and more, he has missed the model of Jesus Christ, he has missed the model of the apostles. Even in the Old Testament, people could possess things. The children of Israel could possess things but the Levites were limited. And the Levites could possess up to some extent but not the priests. The priests could possess up to a certain extent. They were free up to a certain extent; but not the high priest. Even he was free up to some extent. Moses, the supreme human leader, was given only the breast of the animal that was sacrificed at the ordination of the high priest. And there were only two of such ordinations in his life. So that's all he had. That's all that was given to him – Set apart to

God, not set apart to man, not set apart to the world; set apart to God.

Another piece of land is another thing to worry about; isn't it? – how to occupy it, how to protect it from being stolen. Another house is another thing to take care of. Each comes with its own worries and leaves you no longer the same. Is that not so, brother? So when God dispossesses a man in order to simplify his life, He has promoted him. Set apart to God; set apart to God.

Judges 13:6-7,

Then the woman went to her husband and told him, 'A man of God came to me. He looked like an angel of God, very awesome. I didn't ask him where he came from, and he didn't tell me his name. But he said to me, 'You will conceive and give birth to a son. Now then, drink no wine or other fermented drink and do not eat anything unclean, because the boy will be a Nazirite of God from birth until the day of his death.'

Please, I'll go one step back. I'll tell you just exactly as God said it during the Jos Convention. I was being spoken to from heaven. The Lord said if somebody has a million francs today, 2007, and invests it into tracts to save the lost, now in 2008 that money in his heavenly bank account will become 10 million because of the souls won.

In 2009, it will be a hundred million.
2010, it will be one billion
2011, it will be 10 billion.
2012 - a hundred billion.
2013 - one thousand billion.
2014 - ten thousand billion.
2015 - 100,000 billion.

2016 - 1,000,000,000,000,000
2017 - 10,000,000,000,000,000

That's how it will be.

2017	10,000,000,000,000,000
2016	1,000,000,000,000,000
2015	100,000,000,000,000
2014	10,000,000,000,000
2013	1,000,000,000,000
2012	100,000,000,000
2011	10,000,000,000
2010	1,000,000,000
2009	100,000,000
2008	10,000,000
2007	1,000,000

He said if the person keeps the money for himself, because all the possessions of a believer really belong to the Lord, that is, if he does not put it into souls, this is what happens when it is not put into souls. 2008, it reduces to a hundred thousand. 2009, then 10,000.

Year		
2017	10,000,000,000,000,000	
2016	1,000,000,000,000,000	
2015	100,000,000,000,000	
2014	10,000,000,000,000	
2013	1,000,000,000,000	
2012	100,000,000,000	1
2011	10,000,000,000	10
2010	1,000,000,000	100
2009	100,000,000	1.000
2008	10,000,000	10,000
2007	1,000,000	100,000

Brethren, having had the privilege to receive such light about finances as seen in heaven, to act differently, I will be like a man whose brains have been changed into "contry achu" (pounded cocoyam tubers). It will be as if a ten-tonne truck ground my brain to pulp. So when I look at things, I see them according to what was shown me from heaven. That is it. That's by keeping, by investment on earth, by carrying out worldly projects in the hope of giving to God someday. If this (one million) is changed into tracts and a hundred thousand tracts are produced, and one thousand tracts lead to the salvation of one person, even if it's that poor, then you'll have a hundred people saved here. And if each one of them wins somebody, next year it'll be 200, 400, 800, and onward endlessly.

Year			
2017		10,000,000,000,000,000	
2016		1,000,000,000,000,000	
2015		100,000,000,000,000	
2014		10,000,000,000,000	
2013		1,000,000,000,000	1
2012		100,000,000,000	10
2011		10,000,000,000	100
2010	800	1,000,000,000	1,000
2009	400	100,000,000	10,000
2008	200	10,000,000	100,000
2007	100	1,000,000	

Lord, trouble the brethren with these facts! Trouble the brethren, with these facts! Trouble the brethren with these facts. Trouble the brethren with the facts! Trouble the brethren with the facts. Trouble the brethren with this light!

It cannot be bought. It cannot be forced on anybody. Finally, each one must act according to what God has told him. You cannot borrow Rhema. It comes out of your walk with God. Not everybody was set aside to be a Nazirite of God. But there are also others who consecrate themselves to be Nazirites for God. They beg God to set them apart.

Why did God use Samson? An unusual life was demanded of his mother and an unusual life was demanded of him.

In Judges 13:12, *So Manoah asked him,*

> *"When your words are fulfilled, what is to be the rule for the boy's life and work?"*

I want you to listen. "What is to be the rule for the boy's life, the rule for the boy's work?'. These people knew the Word. They knew that leadership could not be separated from the rules – rules for life and rules for Ministry. They asked; then –

The angel of the LORD answered, 'Your wife must do all that I have told her. She must not eat anything that comes from the grapevine, nor drink any wine or other fermented drink nor eat anything unclean. She must do everything I have commanded he.' (Judges 13:13-14).

Do you see three musts? "Your wife must do all that I have told her. She must not eat anything that comes from the grapevine, nor drink any wine or other fermented drink nor eat anything unclean. She must do everything I have commanded her."

By three unchanging musts, Samson's mother was set apart to give birth to this leader.

Permit me to come back to my father. When my father was first posted away from his people, there was a tribe on the way to the tribe where he was sent. Our people believed that these people were cannibals. I won't bring the names in. It was like "Etoug-Ebe" and then "The Etoug-Ebe of Eaters of People." He was sent beyond the land of "The Eaters of People." That was his reward for refusing 18 pence and choosing one penny. When he said he was going, his father cried; his mother cried; his wife, my mother, cried. He said, "OK, keep crying." He went out and set out. After three months, he was back. And he went and went and went and went and went. He hardly passed by the village. When he was posted back to the village, he died the following year. Had he not been sent back, he would not have died. In the days then when the Presbyterian Church was on fire, where you came from did not matter. This thing of beginning to say, "Go back to your village because you are getting old" is a policy of a backslidden condition. I am fully convinced that if our father was not sent back to Moghamo, he would have lived very many years. You must be very careful how others influence you. You must resist their calling you away from your conse-cration.

"What is to be the rule of life and the rule of Ministry?" I want to say that I've been working on this since 1987. It was during the first 40-day fast that I wrote the first document on my Separation from the Common because I began to know that I was born to wear chains or fail.

So Samson's mother was in chains. Samson was born to be in chains. You know, as a Nazirite, Samson was not to touch a dead body. His hair was to be unshaven. He was not to touch a dead body. His hair was not cut.

Judges 13:24,

> *The woman gave birth to a boy and named him Samson. He grew and the LORD blessed him.*

There was a foundation on which the blessings of God could fall - the foundation of a mother set aside, a woman in chains. So the blessing of God came on Samson and the Spirit of the Lord began to stir him. When he tore the lion, on his return he found honey. He scooped it out with his hands. Judges 14:9a,

> *He scooped it out with his hands.*

He touched a dead body. He touched a dead body. He touched a dead body. In scooping with his hand, Oh, he was violating his Separation from the Common! He was violating his Separation from the Common because of food, because of food, just as Adam and Eve abandoned their Separation from the Common because of food. How food has tested people! How food has tested people, tried them, and buried many. How, much has been sacrificed on the altar of food!

From Sierra Leone I had to phone that a certain sister be warned because I was before the Lord when He told me. "I'm angry! I'm angry! I'm angry! I'm angry!" She stopped the fast on Friday and she's already committing gluttony. By the grace of God, somebody phoned me through whom I could send the message to give this glutton.

That was the first temptation – food. But he did not lose all there. What he lost was his relationship with God and not the power of God upon him. The greatest thing about a man or a woman is not power; it is the place in God's heart. The greatest thing about a man is not God's power flowing through him; it is his place in God's heart. Samson lost something of the relationship with God but he maintained his power.

His hair was not to be cut. Can you imagine it? When people saw him he looked like a wild animal – his hair since birth. And if his hair grew fast, he must have looked weird. While he looked weird when it was necessary, Oh the Holy Spirit came upon him in power! The Holy Spirit came upon him in power! The Holy Spirit came upon him in power! And he maintained this weirdness for many years.

In Judges 14: 6a,

> *The Spirit of the Lord came upon him in power!"* Verse 19a, *The Spirit of the Lord came upon him in power!* Chapter 15 verse 14b, *The Spirit of the Lord came upon him in power!*

He was a man who knew a triple anointing. So God used Samson to impose leadership and maintain it because he was separated from the Common.

You may ask, "What does God benefit from hair that makes a man look strange?" Don't ask me. God wants it. And we know when he became normal with regards to his hair, he became weak like any other man. If God gives you very specific instructions, don't take them to the bar of logic. If Samson asked, "What is this much hair for? Is that power?" When He told Ezekiel to lie for 390 days, to eat food that is cooked on human excrement – you may want to ask, "What is wrong with God?" OK, ask. Don't obey. He will not suffer loss. You will be the loser.

For Adam, he had said, "I've been told to eat all fruits except this one. Why is there this exception?" He asked and he ate, and the consequences continue to this day. God is God. When He has spoken, He has spoken!

I thank God for the privilege of preaching what I preached last week and three weeks ago about the vows and the Separation from the Common because these have constituted the fiercest battles of my life. I sealed all today and I wept. Now that I can no longer receive gifts except food, hospitality, transportation and books, I wept specially because of Ruth. She's the one who will suffer the greatest loss because she can't give me gifts any longer. I tried to reason; I said, "God, but I give the gifts away." I said, "I sell some and give You the money." I told Him "For two years, I've given all the cash gifts to You." He said, "Zach Fomum, you are speaking like a mad man! Stop it!" And I stopped. It's madness to talk to God this way. It is madness to try to teach God logic. If He's God then He's to be obeyed. I've obeyed. I will obey. And I beg you to help me obey. The reasons will not be obvious soon. The miraculous provisions will not come immediately. The extraordinary healings will not come immediately; so that I have enough time to go back if I want to. But I'm not going back. Just look in the next few years – one, two, three years –

and whoever suffers today will testify then that it was glorious to have obeyed.

And brethren, don't call me "Daddy." If I give you a Certificate of Adoption, you may. For every other person, I'm Zacharias Tanee Fomum, brother Zach or Professor Fomum. I was strictly forbidden. Now that I'm putting everything right, I will not leave one stone unturned. The biological children can. Adopted children can because they are equivalent in every way to the biological children but I must give you a Certificate of Adoption because it's a covenant.

The embracing of people has ended. I've worked on a lot of the other things that are inward. It's been the battle of the last two years but the special battle of the last three months and since the fast began, God has helped me to go most rapidly.

I would rather die than lie; I will speak all the truth. If I had to hide one fact and gain the whole world, I would not hide it; I will not keep quiet, behaving as if I don't know what I know. The standards of heaven will be brought to bear on everything, even on the academic. I shall never say something behind somebody's back that will hurt his reputation. Don't come and tell me, "This is between both of us." Everything you tell me, I will tell people; so, know it. But if you confess your sins to me, they will never be disclosed. If you confess your failure, it will end there. Don't come and talk to me about your husband or about your child or about anyone.

From this day, I declare myself absolutely loyal to the Head of State, absolutely loyal to the government. If you think differently, don't mention it in my ears. If something is not going, don't say it to me. God has a blueprint for this nation and that blueprint is the prophecy that came with the overthrow of the Prince of Cameroon. I believe it to the dot. Those who attended the Cameroon leaders' Meeting last year, God told us we were to speak to the dry bones, isn't it so? We have not obeyed. We have put on carnal eyes and looked around and spoken what we ought to be ashamed of. If you don't know there is a document: "Prophecy of the Overthrow of the Satanic Prince of Cameroon." There will emerge a new nation that will not come about by condemning any leader or speaking evil but just by saying what God said He would do, proclaiming what God said He would do. That's what you are to say to God. Regardless of what you see to the right, what you see to the left, say to God what God said. Say to God what God said. If we had practised it since we met here in May last year, we would be very far ahead indeed.

Ezekiel 37: 1-3a,

> *The hand of the LORD was upon me, and he brought me out by the Spirit of the LORD and set me in the middle of a valley; it was full of bones. He led me to and fro among them, and I saw a great many bones on the floor of the valley, bones that were very dry. He asked me, 'Son of man, can these bones live?'*

Brother, can these bones live? Brother, can these bones live? Brother, can these bones live? Brother, can these bones live? It is not a superficial question. The prophet refused to commit himself. (Verse 3b)

> *I said, 'O Sovereign LORD, you alone know.'*

No, I don't speak like that. I am a New Testament prophet. "The Spirit of the Lord is upon me."

(Verse 3 a),

> *Son of man, can these bones live?*

They not only can, they will live!

(Verse 4),

> *Then he said to me, Prophesy to these bones and say to them, "Dry bones, hear the word of the LORD! Dry bones, hear the word of the Lord!"*

This is what I will be doing every Wednesday, (Pages 8-11, paragraph 2):

Cameroon.

Cameroon.

Cameroon.

Cameroon.

Cameroon.

Cameroon.

A lofty nation.

A lofty nation.

A lofty nation.

A lofty nation.

A lofty nation.

A lofty nation.

Great! A great nation!

Great! A great nation!

Great! A great nation!

Great! A great nation!

Great!A great nation!

Great!A great nation!

Great before Me, great before man.

Prosperous before Me, prosperous before men.

Prosperous before Me.

Prosperous according to the prosperity of Heaven.

Prosperous according to the prosperity of Heaven.

Prosperous according to the prosperity of Heaven.

Prosperous according to the prosperity of Earth.

Prosperous, prosperous, prosperous.

A nation, a nation where My holiness is established.

A nation where My Kingdom comes.

A nation where My Kingdom comes.

A nation where My Kingdom comes.

A nation where My Kingdom comes.

A nation where My Kingdom comes.

A nation where My Kingdom comes.

And a nation where My will is done

And a nation where My will is done

And a nation where My will is done.

And a nation where My will is done

And a nation where My will is done

And a nation where My will is done.

A nation where My will is done as in Heaven

Done, done, done on Earth as in Heaven;

So that the prosperity of Heaven and the prosperity of Earth might hold together.

So that the prosperity of Heaven and the prosperity of Earth might hold together.

So that the prosperity of Heaven and the prosperity of Earth might hold together.

Might hold together.

Might hold together

Might hold together; so that there will be joy in Heaven and joy on Earth

Cameroon. Cameroon, Cameroon

A nation of My prosperity

A nation of My prosperity

A nation of My prosperity

A nation of My prosperity

A nation of abundance, abundance, abundance, abundance, abundance

And there shall be abundance.

And there shall be abundance.

And there shall be abundance

And there shall be abundance.

And there will be My abundance

And there will be My abundance.

And there will be My abundance.

The abundance of hearts after Me.

The abundance of hearts that seek Me.

The abundance of hearts that find Me.

The abundance of hearts that love Me.

The abundance that wants the way of Heaven.

The abundance of the thirst for Heaven.

The abundance of the things of Heaven.

Abundance, abundance, abundance and abundance and abundance and abundance.

Abundance of righteousness.

Abundance of peace.

Abundance of righteousness - abundance, abundance, abundance.

And there shall be abundance, abundance, abundance.

My abundance, My abundance, My abundance, My abundance

My abundance, My abundance, My abundance, My abundance

My abundance, My abundance, My abundance, My abundance

My abundance, My abundance, My abundance, My abundance

My abundance, My abundance, My abundance, My abundance

My abundance, My abundance, My abundance, My abundance

My abundance, My abundance, My abundance, My abundance

My abundance, My abundance, My abundance, My abundance

And there shall be blessing.

And there shall be blessing.

And there shall be blessing.

And so on.

I want to thank the Lord for His restraining Hand. We have not sent out another bulletin after this one. That's how we are to invite people back to this. We are going to intercede until the heavens open upon the nation.

Pages 14 (paragraph 2) -15 (end of page):

And I will bring My harmony in the nation.

And there shall be peace from the extreme North to the extreme South

And then from the extreme East to the extreme West.

And then Cameroon shall live in peace.

And then Cameroon shall live in peace.

And then Cameroon shall live in peace.

And then Cameroon shall live in peace

And I will ignore tribal differences.

And I will put aside tribal differences.

And there shall be harmony.

And there shall be harmony.

And there shall be harmony.

And there shall be harmony.

And I will lift the nation from the sin of greed.

And the Cameroonians shall begin to think of each other.

And the Cameroonians shall begin to think of each other.

And the Cameroonians shall begin to think of each other.

And the Cameroonians shall begin to think of each other.

And the Cameroonians shall begin to help each other.

And the Cameroonians shall begin to help each other.

And the Cameroonians, unlike at the present, will begin to feel for each other.

They shall begin to feel for each other.

And they shall lift each other and they shall encourage each other.

And they shall share My blessings, and they shall share My blessings.

And they shall share My blessings, and they shall share My blessings.

And they shall share My blessings, and they shall share My blessings.

And they shall share My blessings, and they shall share My blessings.

And the Northerner shall share My blessing with the Southerner.

And the Easterner will share My blessings with the Westerner.

And there will be a harmony created in My very bosom and imparted to the nation

And imparted to the nation.

And imparted to the nation.

And imparted to the nation

And there will be blessing

And there will be blessing

And there will be blessing

And there will be harmony

And there will be harmony

And there will be harmony

And there will be justice.

And there will be justice.

And there will be justice.

And there will be satisfaction.

And there will be satisfaction.

And there will be satisfaction.

The way of obedience is the way of gain. I just beg you, brother, just obey. God will handle the rest. Please, I want to plead with you. Since we don't see beyond now, let's just obey and the Lord will handle things that are days and weeks and months ahead. Pray. I want you to receive a spirit of obedience, an anointing to obey the Lord. On the 28th day of the Fast, the Lord told me that the next 28 days will be easier than easy. When God says a thing, lay hold on it. When God says a thing, lay hold on it. When God says a thing, lay hold on it. We command you to be aggressive people who are laying hold on what God says. Believe God! Believe His Word! Believe yourself!

Listen, brother; if you doubt God, how will you believe man? If you doubt yourself, how will you believe another? If you don't believe God crazily, then you will doubt man and doubt yourself.

WHY GOD CHOOSES CERTAIN PEOPLE—THE FIRST THREE KINGS OF ISRAEL

Why did God choose the people who were the first three kings of Israel? - Saul, David and Solomon

Tuesday, 27th February, 2007.

The first thing we said was that appointment to leadership is a divine prerogative. And we began to ask the question: "Why did God choose some and not others?" Let us look at why God choose the people who were the first three kings of Israel. Later on, it was a matter of succession but from the beginning God chose people who met some requirements.

Let's look at the first king. Why did God choose Saul? He was the Number One man. You cannot lead from behind. The leader is ahead. He must provide a leadership gap. If the people are here (lower rungs), the leader must be there (far above) so that they look at him far ahead and follow him.

Leader

People

If he's at the same level as they are, he's dishonest to call himself their leader. He's dishonest to expect them to follow him.

1Samuel 9:1-2,

> *There was a Benjaminite, a man of standing, whose name was Kish son of Abiel, the son of Zeror, the son of Becorath, the son of Aphiah of Benjamin. He had a son named Saul, an impressive young man without equal among the Israelites – a head taller than any of the others.*

Without equal; he was the Number One man. There were no two people to select from. He was the Number One man. The leader must be the Number One man, if he's not, he's dishonest. Leadership will be taken out of his hands. There's no question about it that leadership will be stripped from the person who goes fooling around, fooling around at the same level as the people When a man stops being the Number One man, he has lost his leadership. "Without equal, without equal, without equal, a head taller than any of the others, a head taller than any of the others." People must ask, "Why should we follow you?" If not, those people are very dishonest. "Why must I follow? Why must I put my all into this man? Why must I follow?" He must have credentials that compel people to follow. He must have credentials that compel the people to follow! His credentials must be such that all honest people follow him easily.

I remember in 1985, I withdrew to Nkolbisson to do my first forty-day fast. After 14 days, my gums were bleeding; I stopped the fast. I thought I would die. Odilia M. had a disciple then. She said, "Ah, he has stopped the fast. He will say it is the devil." And she left the Church because I had failed. I even went to her house near EMIA (Inter-Army Military School). I even went there to convince her to come back. She didn't come back. But I got the message. People will not follow a leadership that fails! The failure of leadership is personal dismissal! I got the message. "Without equal."

In 1Samuel 10:24a,

> *Samuel said to all the people, 'Do you see the man the LORD has chosen? There is no-one like him among all the people.*

The Lord chooses the person who is above all the people or who will soon be above them and who will increasingly be above them. Verse 24b, *There is no-one like him among all the people.*

Then the people shouted, 'Long live the king!" And Saul was capable of great deeds. When these Ammonites mocked, 1Samuel 11:6-8,

> *When Saul heard their words, the Spirit of God came upon him in power, and he burned with anger. He took a pair of oxen, cut them into pieces, and sent the pieces by messengers throughout Israel, proclaiming, "This is what will be done to the oxen of anyone who*

does not follow Saul and Samuel." Then the terror of the LORD fell on the people, and they turned out as one man. When Saul mustered them at Bezek, the men of Israel numbered three hundred thousand and the men of Judah thirty thousand.

The people follow the man upon whom the Holy Spirit falls. In 1Samuel 10:10a, the Bible says,

When they arrived at Gibeah, a procession of prophets met him (i.e. Saul)*; the Spirit of God came upon him in power.*

The leader is the one upon whom the Holy Spirit comes in power, and if need be, a second time, if need be, a third time. So the Spirit came upon him there and then, in Chapter 11. The Holy Spirit came upon him. There must be undeniable proof that "God has chosen this one." The people must name the things about which they cannot see "the back of his head.[1]" They must acknowledge, "God has made this one to be ahead of us."

Listen; when God found someone better than Saul, the leadership changed hands. In 1 Samuel 15:28,

Samuel said to him, 'The LORD has torn the kingdom of Israel from you today and has given it to one of your neighbours – to one better than you.

There was now one better than he. In the next chapter there's another leader appointed. When someone better than you rises, your leadership before God has ended. "Another one better than you." There was now one better than him. And the Spirit of God left him and rested upon the better one and an evil spirit troubled him.

Pray that this lesson would sink.

You can work to get to the top. You can work to qualify. Even in the natural it is said that 1% of the leaders are born; 99% are made.

Let's move on to David. Why David was made leader? He started early by an unusual relationship with his father. He was a loyalist to his father. I want to say, a wrong attitude to one's father is one of the greatest handicaps a man can carry all his life. Putting it in other words, the father is the king-maker. I've studied many people since I knew some of these things. I found that they were untrue to their fathers. They were disloyal. It's a heavy handicap. One thing that God does in preparing people for future leadership is to give them the right attitude towards their natural fathers. Look at Ham, the son who exposed his father's nakedness; he was cursed. His heart was wrong towards his father and he earned a curse. I don't know anybody who disobeyed their father and did not suffer. The father might have been an unbeliever. When you see a great man, go and see what happened between his father and him. When you see a great woman, go and see what happened between her father and her. When you see great-ness slipping out of people's hands, go and trace it in what happened between their fathers and they. If there is some-thing that you can do about your relationship with your father, do it. If not, I want to tell you; when you will be 60, you will be weeping over it. You will see greatness slipping out of your hands. It will follow you. That you can rebel against your father means that the devil has chosen you to fail. It doesn't matter what your father is; that you can oppose him, is saying that there is a curse on you to destroy you. When you will be 40, 50, 60, 70, you will confront it. I could give you two hundred examples. If you are the one who causes your father pain, you will receive it a million times. It is dras-tic. How can I put it? You know, your father does not know.

Your father does not know that he's wrong and you are right. But you have your whole life to live it and to be sorry, to regret, to be bitter, when you will see things just slip out of your hands.

Brother, I wish I could whisper this lesson into the ears of every child and after that, into the ears of every spiritual child. If your attitude to your spiritual father is wrong, you must fail. You may think that you have succeeded but you have ruined a lot. Your attitude to your spiritual father - if you are disloyal, you don't follow him, you don't exalt him, you are not his servant, I want to tell you, you must fail. You can say, "The other one was physical, this one is spiritual." You might be destined to great heights; you will not get there. Criticize him. Each criticism of him in your heart is a curse upon yourself. Each reservation is a curse! Each putting aside of what he says is a curse! I wish I could just sit with twelve people to give them three hundred examples. Brethren, a man treats his spiritual father badly exactly in the way he treats his natural father so as to compound the curse, unless he has faced the Cross and repented in sackcloth and ashes.

If I were a young man looking for a girl to marry, I would flee from any girl who has a wrong relationship with her father. If I were a young girl looking for a man, I would be single rather than marry a boy who has a wrong relationship with his father. There is no future for the marriage. It may look wonderful but it will be heartache, heartache, heartache.

Let me take another domain. I would not be where I am today in Science but for the fact that I was blessed with a perfect heart attitude towards Professor Landor. God is my witness, I never murmured in my heart for once against him – never. The God of heaven is my Witness. That's where I got my greatness. And more is coming. When I got to Kampala on 15th October 1969, I shared a very big laboratory with a man. I will withhold his name because it's not positive. He already had an MSc. by research. I came there as a fresh BSc. student. This man complained against the Professor everyday. After four years, he went away with nothing. The other one who was in the other laboratory had a Masters degree from London. He got his Ph.D. seven years after I had had mine. He was another complainant. I will give one more example. There was another one who specialised in looking for the Professor's faults. He came in six months after me. We have just put his name on an article we are jointly publishing. He collected the plant for us in Uganda. It is his second publication. I have over 130. We were in the same laboratory with the same supervisor. Recently, when I was in Uganda he came to tell me the story of his life - his wrong attitude to Professor Landor. What is in the heart finally comes out. Professor Landor asked him to come to the West Indies and finish his work. The day he was leaving, he said he drank and publicly took sides with Professor Landor's opponents. But it's something that started already many years before. That is life – the attitude towards the academic father. Everywhere you go, you meet a father – for your blessing or your cursing.

There's a Nigerian pastor who teaches the matter of fatherhood in depth, breadth and height. He's based in the U.S. I listened to him once and I will be eternally grateful to him. He said he went round in circles for ten years in his ministry until the truth of fatherhood dawned upon him. He had believed in the Scripture Union. He sought a spiritual father. He sought a spiritual father. The day he was accepted, he burst into tears of joy. And the next year, his Ministry blew up tenfold. That was the missing link.

Look for a father. Look for a spiritual father. Be adopted formally. If for some reason you don't have a biological father or you don't know him, get adopted, get adopted. You need a father. Your children need a grandfather. If not, there are some things that you cannot have and they cannot have. You need a father. You can be struggling to manage but it will not work. You can go up to some point but there will be telling gaps in your being, in your children, in your spiritual children.

There was a school for David. It was the school of his father, Jesse. It's in that school that the greatest king of Israel was trained. Around 16 or 17, as a shepherd taking care of his father's flock, out of his singular love for his father, he developed the skills that raised him to greatest heights

> *So Saul said to his attendants, 'Find someone who plays well and bring him to me.'*
>
> *One of the servants answered, 'I have seen a son of Jesse of Bethlehem who knows how to play the harp. He is a brave man and a warrior. He speaks well and is a fine-looking man. And the Lord is with him.'*

He said, "I've seen the son of Jesse." He didn't say, 'I've seen David" or "A son of Jesse."

1 Samuel 17:55 – 58,

> *As Saul watched David going out to meet the Philistine, he said to Abner, commander of the army, " Abner, whose son is that young man?"*
>
> *Abner replied. "As surely as you live, O king, I don't know."*
>
> *The king said, "Find out whose son this young man is."*
>
> *As soon as David returned from killing the Philistine, Abner took him and brought him before Saul, with David still holding the Philistine's head.*

"Whose son are you, young man?" Saul asked him.

David said. "I am the son of your servant Jesse of Bethlehem."

In the school of his father, he learnt how to play the harp, he learnt bravery, he fought against lions, against bears, and the Lord was with him. David's greatness was cultivated while he served as a shepherd. There was no one there. Alone in the fields, he could have done whatever he wanted. Why did he risk his life when lions came? – Because of his love for his father. He was loyal to his father. And he risked his life for his father's flock. When a lion came to attack he could have said, "O, let the lion take what it wants; let me save my life." But he risked his life for his father's sake. He would go after the lion, and kill it. Even when it had carried a goat away, he would go after it thus risking his life. He would go after it and smite it. When it turned against him, he took it by the beard, hit it and knocked the life out of it. The school of being a son, a loyal son, a son who counted his father's interest of greater importance to him than his own life.

The Nigerian in his lecture said, "You must consider your father's ministry as your own and forget your own ministry and work for your father's ministry. God will raise people to work for your own ministry." He spoke to us. He said that the first thing he still does in the year is to take the January tithe of his ministry, all the money that comes to him in January in his ministry and give it to his father—the man he made his spiritual father.

Do you see the same spirit in Joseph? Joseph bought all the land for Pharaoh. He got all the money for Pharaoh and then he got all the Egyptians as slaves for Pharaoh. He was a son. And he prospered. All his brothers who were murmuring against their father, jealous of their brother, obviously complaining about the father, who wounded their father in the way they treated Joseph, limited their progress.

That was the heart of David. Even when his brothers went to war, his father sent him to them. He was close to his father. He was his father's servant. He was available. He was his father's errand-boy. And, of course, the Holy Spirit came upon him. 1 Samuel 16:11-13a,

> *So he asked Jesse, "Are these all the sons you have?"*
>
> *"There is still the youngest." Jesse answered, "but he is tending the sheep."*
>
> *Samuel said. "Send for him; we will not sit down until he arrives."*
>
> *So he sent and had him brought in. He was ruddy, with a fine appearance and handsome features.*
>
> *Then the LORD said, "Rise and anoint him; he is the one."*
>
> *So Samuel took the horn of oil and anointed him in the presence of his brothers, and from that day on the Spirit of the LORD came upon David in power.*

"From that day" – it means that there was repeated anointing. "From that day the Holy Spirit came upon him in power." That's why God chose him. In 2Samuel 8 we read about David's victories.

> Verse 1-4, *In the course of time, David defeated the Philistines and subdued them, and he took Metheg Ammah from the control of the Philistines.*
>
> *David also defeated the Moabites. He made them lie down on the ground and measured them off with a length of cord. Every two lengths of them were put to death, and the third length was allowed*

to live. So the Moabites became subject to David and brought tribute.

Moreover, David fought Hadadezer, son of Rehob, king of Zobah, when he went to restore his control along the Euphrates River. David captured a thousand of his chariots, seven thousand charioteers and twenty thousand foot soldiers. He hamstrung all but a hundred of the chariot horses.

Verses 5-6,

When the Arameans of Damascus came to help Hadadezer king of Zobah, David struck down twenty-two thousand of them. He put garrisons in the Aramean kingdom of Damascus, and the Arameans became subject to him and brought tribute. The LORD gave David victory wherever he went."

Verse 7-8,

David took the gold shields that belonged to the officers of Hadadezer and brought them to Jerusalem. From Tebah and Berothai, towns that belonged to Hadadezer, King David took a great quantity of bronze.

And so on.

Verse 11,

King David dedicated these articles to the Lord, as he had done with the silver and gold from all the nations he had subdued.

Why did God choose him? All he acquired, he gave to God. All he acquired, he gave to God. All he acquired, he gave to God. All he acquired, he gave to God. David made God rich. A man who impoverishes God cannot be appointed to leadership. If he is appointed, he will soon be removed. The power to give to God, the power to give to God, the power to give to God flows from a good heart – The giving to God! The giving to God! The giving to God! The giving to God! The giving to God! The giving to God! The giving to God!

It says in Verse 12,

> *Edom and Moab, the Ammonites and the Philistines, and Amalek. He also dedicated the plunder taken from Hadadezer son of Rehob, king of Zobah.*

Today you give a big percentage; the next day you give a lower percentage to God, playing with God at risk of dismantling your leadership or ensuring that God never makes you a leader. Your eye is on your own interest. Your eye is not on His interests. You want to build your own kingdom, build your projects so that His suffer loss. O poor man, you will not prosper! God appoints to leadership the people who will persistently and continuously put divine interests ahead of personal ones. It's not doing it once; it's not doing it occasionally. It is a permanent bent in that direction. That's what God is looking for. It's not that today you put God first, tomorrow you put yourself first, tomorrow you put God first, the next day you put yourself first. It is a permanent stance that says, "My projects will suffer loss. My projects will suffer loss. His must never suffer loss." And those who honour Him, He honours.

The Lord gave David victory wherever he went. That's why God chose him He looked at David's heart and said, "This man is a man after My own heart. This man is a man after My own heart".

What does God say about you? What does God say about you? What does God say about you? "A man after My own heart.

David gave to God at three levels.

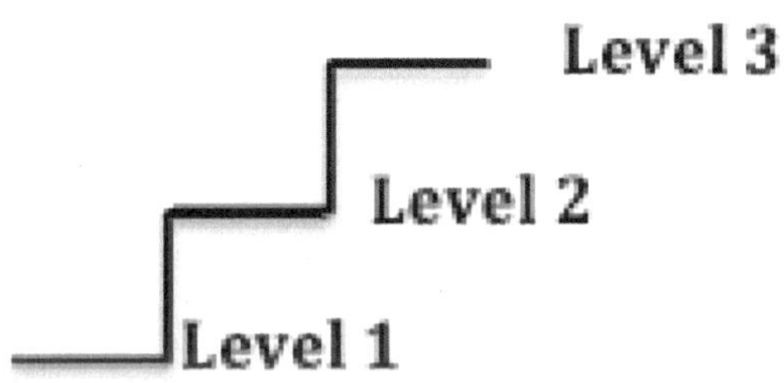

In 1Chronicles 29:2,

With all my resources I have provided for the temple of my God - gold for the gold work, silver for the silver, bronze for the bronze, iron for the iron and wood for the wood, as well as onyx for the settings, turquoise, stones of various colours, and all kinds of fine stone and marble - all of these in large quantities.

That's Level One.

Second level – Verses 3 and 4a. He says,

Besides, in my devotion to the temple of my God.

Now as a worshipper, as a lover, O, as the man after God's heart, as the man after God's heart, as the man after God's heart, he says,

In my devotion to the temple of my God I now give my personal treasures of gold and silver for the temple of my God, over and above everything I have provided for this holy temple.

"My devotion, my God, my personal treasure, my God" – Brethren, do you see the intimacy? The intimacy, you see the intimacy, these hearts that fused, that bonded, and that overflowed. That's Level 2. What did he give at that level?

"Three thousand talents of gold, (the gold of Ophir)" – That's first class gold. "And seven thousand talents of refined silver," – Not just silver - refined silver (Verse 4b).

Then he moves to Level 3.

1 Chronicles 22:14, King James Version:

> *Now, behold, in my trouble I have prepared for the house of the Lord an hundred thousand talents of gold, and a thousand thousand talents of silver; and of brass and iron without weight; for it is in abundance: timber also and stone have I prepared; and thou mayest add to.*

Revised Standard Version:

> *With great pains I have provided for the house of the Lord a hundred thousand talents of gold, a million talents of silver, and bronze and iron beyond weighing, for there is so much of it; timber and stone too I have provided. To these you must add.*

"With great pains" - it was now giving to the Lord in the millions. The quantity was great beyond measure. But it was giving that wounded him. It smashed his own projects. It ruined his own projects. He bled to provide for his God. By so doing, he rose to the commander's level – To this you must add!" He could now command. "You must add!" He was now a commander through bleeding giving.

If you are not a leader in your giving, you are sick beyond measure. God will not exalt you. God will not bless your leadership. In fact, He will crumble it because you will ruin His cause. The people give as their leader gives because money is so important for the Kingdom of God. We have not produced a tract for a long time; we don't have the money. When a leader does not provide a model in giving so that the people might follow his model, he has buried God's cause and God must demote him.

"With great pains" - The giving broke his heart, broke his projects And it raised him to the rank of a commander. "To this you must add!"

After David gave in 1Chronicles 29 he then asked,

> *Now, who is willing to consecrate himself today to the LORD?* (Verse 5b).

The Bible says,

> *Then the leaders of families, the officers of the tribes of Israel, the commanders of thousands and commanders of hundreds, and the officials in charge of the king's work gave willingly* (Verse 6).

They had a model to follow. Listen, brethren, they knew what David had given. There's something wrong in a man whose giving is not known. David spelt it out. It was not giving to the poor. It was not giving to the poor where they say the left hand should not know what the right hand is giving. This was giving to his God and he mentioned it in clear detail, told them the details clearly – the quantities of what he gave in all three passages. That's why God chose him. He knew he would keep nothing for himself. We said God chooses a man, God chooses a Leader, "a neighbour of yours who is better than you."

Why did God choose Solomon? Normally everything was against Solomon becoming king. You know where he came from. Why did God choose him? To put it in human terms, it was not possible for God not to choose him because we have said a leader is exceptionally great. He makes everybody else look small so that they might follow because they cannot follow from the same level. He must be so far ahead the people that they struggle to see him. In a book that I read, it said,

> *"The leader must be the One whose deeds*
> *cause the ears to tingle. You mention this*
> *astounding area of his life, it's success.*
> *And you think that's all. You mention*
> *another, you find another astounding one.*
> *You think that's all. You mention another*
> *..."*

This was written in a secular book.

Exodus 35:30-33,

> *Then Moses said to the Israelites, 'See, the Lord has chosen Bezalel son of Uri, the son of Hur, of the tribe of Judah, and he has filled him with the Spirit of God, with skill, ability and knowledge in all kinds of crafts - to make artistic designs for work in gold, silver and bronze, to cut and set stones, to work in wood and to engage in all kinds of artistic craftsmanship.*

Look at the whole domain of his competence—gold, silver, bronze, to cut, to set stones, to work in wood, to engage in all kinds of artistic craftsmanship. In addition - the ability to teach others. That's the leader. He must, by ruthless investment, deepen, broaden, heighten his supremacy so that honest people would follow him and jealous people would not follow him to their undoing. It must be such that any honest man says, "This man must be followed. He's more than I." Bezalel was more than the others. It does not just happen. It is worked upon because it takes years to become a leader, and it takes years to establish your leadership – years in which you accede to heights, might, splendour, greatness and that which commands people to follow. Then honest people will follow you and dishonest people will oppose you to their undoing. There was no one like him. Permit me just to say one thing, brethren. The Spirit of the Lord came upon Bezalel.

Listen, brethren, I worked in Kampala between eighteen and twenty hours everyday in the laboratory. Brethren, I weighed 59 kilos then and I got no results. For twelve months I got no results. Brethren, after the Holy Spirit had come upon me, within three months we produced enough results for three full papers in Perkin. I had seven papers for publication from my PhD thesis. The day the Holy Spirit came upon me, something happened in the laboratory. I became another man. O brethren, the Holy Spirit does not come to possess a man just to fill the spiritual. Everything is altered. Everything is altered. Everything is altered. Professor Landor does not know till this day what happened – that from one day to another, everything just changed. The power of the Holy Spirit came upon me and everything was altered

For Bezalel, he was anointed.

He has filled him with the Spirit of God (Verse 3la).

Now this is what (Samuel) Chadwick said in *The Way to Pentecost*:

"I owe everything to the gift of Pentecost; it came to me when I was not seeking it. I was about my heavenly Father's business; seeking means whereby I could do the work He had called and sent me to do. And in my search I came across a prophet, heard a testimony and set out to seek I knew not what. I knew it was a bigger thing than I had ever known. It came along the line of duty in a crisis of obedience, in a crisis of obedience. When it came, I could not explain what had happened. But I was aware of things unspeakable and full of glory. Some results were immediate. There came into my soul a deep peace, a thrilling joy and a new sense of power." Listen, my mind was quickened. I felt that I had received a new faculty of understanding.

Every power was vitalised. My body powers were quickened.

Take away the Holy Spirit and what I am doing here on the fifty-first day will not be possible. Brethren, I am operating in a totally different power. I am full of energy and I am leaving for the tenth country since the fast started because the power of the Holy Spirit touches not only the spiritual; it touches natural energy.

"My body powers were quickened. There was a new sense of spring and vitality, a new power of endurance and a strong man's exhilaration over big things. Things began to happen. What we had failed to do by strenuous endeavours came to pass without labour. It was as when the Lord Jesus came into the boat that having rowed for long making little progress that immediately the ship was at the land whither they went. It was gloriously wonderful. The things that happened with the least part of the experience (what happened immediately was the least part), the wind, the fire and the tongues aroused many comments, but they vanished. And it was the realities that remained that were most wonderful. The experience gave me the key to all my thinking, all my service, all my life. Pentecost gave me the key to the Scriptures. It has kept me on my feet in all slippery places. The things that are stumbling blocks to so many are stepping stones to me. The inexplicable becomes plain when we recognise the presence and law of the Spirit. It surpasses scholarship and gives discernment beyond all human learning. Indeed, learning without the Holy Spirit blinds men to realities of divine truth." (*From The Way to Pentecost*)

Solomon, why did God choose him?

1 Kings 4:29-34,

> *God gave Solomon wisdom and very great insight, and a breadth of understanding as measureless as the sand on the seashore. Solomon's wisdom was greater than the wisdom of all the men of the East, and greater than all the wisdom of Egypt. He was wiser than any other man, including Ethan the Ezrahite – wiser than Heman, Calcol and Darda, the sons of Mahol. And his fame spread to all the surrounding nations. He spoke three thousand proverbs and his songs numbered a thousand and five. He described plant life, from the cedar of Lebanon to the hyssop that grows out of walls. He also taught about animals and birds, reptiles and fish. Men of all nations came to listen to Solomon's wisdom, sent by all the kings of the world, who had heard of his wisdom.*

Not to have made him king regardless of his origins would have been folly. He was the Number One man.

I want to tell you that you are where you are by choice. When you can fast for seven days, you fast for three days, you have made a choice. When you can fast for ten days, you fast for seven, you have made a choice. When you can fast for twenty-one days, you fast for fourteen. When you can fast for twenty-eight days, you fast for twenty-one. Listen, my beloved, you are where your choices over the years have placed you. When you can give 30%, you give 20, when you can pray for two nights, you pray for one, when you can plant two Churches, you plant one, when you can read your Bible thrice, you read it once, the future is settled.

Brethren, if I were looking for reasons to stop this fast, I would have stopped. On one of the trips, I fell as I was boarding the plane. I was dizzy and then I kicked the stairs. How do I talk to you, brethren? First of all, to the leaders who have cursed their leadership by limiting themselves and not rising to God's heights saying to themselves, "I cannot do this, I cannot do that, I cannot do the other " – God will do to you according to what He hears you say. Your prayer nights have now become nights of sleeping at home. You have made a choice. I want you to know that you have chosen for your children and your grandchildren and your great-grandchildren. They will do what their father did. They will do what their mother did.

WHY GOD CHOOSES CERTAIN PEOPLE—PETER

Why God chooses people to lead: The case of Peter

Tuesday, 6th March, 2007

Why would God choose Peter? By nature, Peter was very hardworking. Lazy people cannot be chosen because as we have said again and again, the leader leads by being ahead. He's a man who has such extraordinary accomplishments that if you are honest, you will want to follow him. There must be extraordinary hard work. Brother, that is your problem, sister, that is your problem. Peter was already the leader of the Galilean Trawlers' Association.

Luke 5:10,

James and John, the sons of Zebedee, Simon's partners.

Peter was already the leader of these people. They were his partners. He was successful in his worldly enterprise. Most believers do not show us proof of success in the things of the world that God has put in their hands. It's mediocrity, mediocrity, mediocrity! Average, average, average! "Pass, pass, pass!" It's a shame! They give the impression that the God of heaven is the God of mediocrity. They bring shame to God's Name by their paltry professional performance. They bring shame to God by their poor academic performance. Everything about them just lacks distinction.

I want to ask you in all honesty: Do your works make you a leader professionally? The marks you got in school, at university, did they say that you are a leader? Peter was a leader. All these people were not his associates when he was behind them. You only complain and complain and complain. You say, "I'm cheated. I'm discriminated against." What distinction have you brought to the place where God put you to work?

I was gladdened yesterday by one of the Nzoyoums. I hear he's 13 or 14. He talked about the assembly in his school. He's leading believers there. So he talks about the assembly in his school. And you, for ten years you can't produce one assembly. And he's always first. You are tailing the class. You started at the same grade and you will retire at the same grade. If people are looking for those who come late, you are always one of them. You have nothing to contribute. Your office is where people gather to criticise. Paralyzed by laziness! I rebuke you in the name of Jesus Christ for being a shame to the Lord Jesus Christ! You say, "I'm waiting for favours, I'm waiting for favours. I'm waiting for favours. I'm waiting for favours."

"I'm waiting for them to look into my case." "They have said that there is a special meeting for "high nines[1]." It is burial of leadership.

Can God's good works be seen through you where God has placed you to work, where God has placed you to study? If you cannot lead unbelievers academically, if you cannot lead unbelievers professionally, how will you lead the people of God? That's the most difficult leadership. Let me tell you, listen, your present spiritual performance may be just a reflection of what your professional performance was or is.

"J'ai tourné, tourné en rond, en rond" (I've gone round in circles.)

"J'ai tourné, tourné ; sans rien faire." (I've gone round and done nothing.)

"J'ai tourné, tourné ; je blâme tout le monde" (I've gone round ; I've blamed everybody.)

Yet the problem is not inability. It is the lack of hard work! Yesterday, you were going like this; today, you have changed direction and are going like that. Tomorrow, you might change and go in another direction. In the name of Jesus Christ, I command you to stop it! The successful person goes in one direction! One direction! One direction! One direction! One direction! One direction! One direction! One direction! One direction! One direction! One direction! One Direction! You are going like this, then you hear people say, "This way or project is attractive." You say, "hmmmmmmm" Then they say, "Here's another attractive one." Listen, brother, you may not know that you are failing. Every new thing is a bait you have been biting. You have not stayed long enough on one thing, on one thing only, for a foundation to be built for progress. What is the area of your specialisation?

There is none. Today you are an electrical engineer, tomorrow you are a construction engineer, the day after you are in aeronautics engineering.

I want to address you brother, with regards to your profession, write down now what your specialisation is. Where must God bring down the blessings? Where is your heart open for the miracle to come? Now turn spiritually. Where must the blessings of God fall? You say, "Well. I want to catch it. If I don't catch it with my toe, I will catch it with my hand, with my stomach." In the Kingdom, what have you given your all to, day in day out for ten years; day in day out for twenty years; day in day out for twenty-five years? Very soon you will switch from this team to join another. You have spent twelve years here and your mad head does not tell you that you are losing, you are losing, you are losing ...' After some time you say, "No, no, no, I am angry, I am angry. I'm leaving this team. There, in the other team, I will not be rebuked." Finally you say, "No, I am in nobody's team I am in the sinking team." You have indeed sunk.

One thing that I've learnt with much heartache and deep regret is to accept someone who leaves a team and joins mine; I have accepted someone who left another person's team and joined mine. Whatever the reasons for their joining mine, if I didn't suffer the first year, I suffered ten years afterwards. In spite of all the wonderful reasons, I want to tell you that in ten years, you'll be very sorry. Send the person back. Brethren, I could give you fifty examples. If somebody dies and people relocate; if you welcome him it's one thing. If a leader leaves a ministry and his people are relocating, it's another thing. But if the person is going strong and someone leaves him and says, "I'm coming over to you," my dear brother, in ten years he will leave you. There's no question about it, regardless of what you do, because it is something wrong in his heart. He's running away from something. In time, he will run away from you. You may look like the cherished one of the moment. You are the cherished fool! Let's verify it in ten years' time. It's like a son who will not submit to his father and says, "I make you my father." If he hit his father with his right hand, he will use a hammer on you. If he didn't love his father, you, who are not even his father, he will hang you. He threw away the blood relationship; and you, what relates you to him? Ah, hang him! Send people to where they belong. You say, "Well, I'm in need." The day they will hang you is the day you will know that you ought not to have been in need. When people say, "Oh, you are wonderful; oh, you provide what my disciple maker does not provide," and the pride of your heart says, "Oh, maybe I'm wonderful Ohhhhh!" I can no longer do what I did in the past having cited examples here and there publicly, but I tell you what will happen: the heart that was disloyal to A will be disloyal to you. The heart that was untrue to A will be untrue to you. The heart that abandoned A will abandon you.

Some years ago, a brother had gone on with a girl for many years. Both parents knew about it. Then he changed his mind for another girl. I was so troubled because for years, the other girl had come to talk to me about their relationship. So I called this new girl. I asked, "What do you think you have that the other girl doesn't have?" She said, "Brother Zach, that girl is hard! This man can never be at home in her presence." Let me not tell you what the same girl now says about the man after some years of marriage to him. You think that you are the angel of tenderness and the other woman is a lioness. Folly! Folly! Folly! Folly! Wait, time will expose you. A man has sworn to his own hurt. Then you say, "I am Miss Tenderness; I will lift him high."

I told the leaders. "As you command relationships to break, I want to warn you. I study human beings. The one who is not contented with A will be doubly discontented with B and triply discontented with C. If you talk clearly to divorcees, they will tell you that their first wives were better. Listen, brethren, it is a domain in which I am a researcher. I've not met one divorcee who says his new wife is better.

When our father died, we went for the burial. My brother was not a believer until the last three weeks of his life. The first woman in my brother's life came and told me, "It is folly that took me away from your brother's house; that made me leave your brother's house and I regret it."

She's not a believer. She says, "That foolishness has haunted me all my life."

So, it is not just hard work; it is consistent hard work in the same direction with regards to persons and with regards to the vision.

Peter could say in Luke 5:5a, *Master, we've worked hard all night.*

That's the man. The first hour they caught nothing; they worked on. The second hour they caught nothing and continued working. The third hour they caught nothing; they kept on working. The fourth hour they caught nothing. Some put in a little effort, then give up; they put in a little effort, then give up. They worked the whole night, the whole night, the whole night, the whole night, the whole night.

Why was Peter chosen? He was a reckless lover of the Lord Jesus Christ in spite of his failures. He loved Jesus Christ with reckless intensity. When they were in the boat and Jesus Christ called out from the shore, Peter could not wait for the boat to slowly get there. He was too much in love with Jesus. He jumped into the water and swam to him. Remember when he walked on the sea before he doubted and started sinking. He was running to Jesus Christ. His heart was burning. His heart was burning. Even when he told Jesus, "Don't go to the Cross," it was foolish love. Peter was aflame with love for the Lord Jesus Christ. Love that is not on fire is no love! Love that is not on fire is no love!

Of our children, Ruth N. loves me. I've never met Ruth and she would not weep with joy to see me. I've never met Ruth and she would not weep because we were parting. Some don't care to see me. If they don't see me for a week, it doesn't matter. If I go for ten days, they will not be there to say, "Welcome." They are cold. Ruth follows me round the world by telephone, emails, everything.

Now I want to ask you, "Is yours cold love or hot love?" Cold love is to be vomited. May God deal with your cold heart! May God deal with your cold heart! Every child who is cold towards the father has chained and limited how far he can rise. Are you cold towards your father? Are you cold towards your mother? Listen, you have decided to curse yourself never to rise to God's heights because as you are cold towards your parents, you will be cold towards your heavenly Father. Maintain a technical relationship. God never blesses technical relationships! God overflows. And all the other relationships - Cold! Cold! Cold! Cold! Cold! Cold! Deep freezer! Or something worse! Where is the father's love? Where is the flame of a father's love? You have a spiritual father; where is the flame? Cold! Cold! Cold! Cold! Cold! Cold! How can God commit great numbers to a cold heart, to somebody in a deep freezer, to a "technicality"?

Peter was chosen because he was hot, hot in his love for the Lord. He would not wait for the formalities – he jumped into the sea and swam fast to Him. And when they wanted to crucify Peter, he said, "No, my Lord was crucified head up. Crucify me with my head down." And that's how he was crucified.

Cold! Cold! Not burning, not yearning. It is impossible to resist burning love. It is written that John was the disciple whom Jesus loved but there is no written record to say that John was the disciple who loved Jesus Christ. Peter was the disciple who loved the Lord, that's why he was chosen. When the Lord called him, Luke 5:11 reads:

So they pulled their boats up on shore, left everything and followed Him.

Peter left everything – his mother-in-law, his wife, his career, everything, and recklessly followed Him. He was married, had a mother-in-law at home but he left everything and followed Jesus. He knew abandonment to Christ that most know nothing about.

Why did the Lord choose Peter? Peter had a tender heart. When he sinned—when he denied the Lord and came back to himself, he wept bitterly, he wept bitterly. He was sensitive to sin. He wept bitterly.

Mark 14:72, the last part:

He broke down and wept.

He broke down and wept. He broke down and wept."

Peter was a broken man. Unbroken men are useless as leaders for God; Peter broke down and he wept. Peter was a weeping leader.

Are you a dry-eyed leader? Dry hearts lead to dry eyes. Dry hearts, dry eyes! Dry hearts, dry eyes! Dry hearts, dry eyes! There is a place in the knowledge of God beyond which dry eyes cannot penetrate. There is a place in intimacy with God that dry eyes cannot reach because the man is unbroken He's limited. There are tears of self-pity. And women have a specialty here; they can produce a bucket for you, or produce tears of rebellion. Again, sisters know how to produce them. They can weep the whole day and night rebelling against you. That's not what we are talking about. I'm talking about tears that flow from intimacy with God or that flow from the knowledge that you have wounded God's heart. Tears are an integral part of intimacy with God. When people fuse into Him, draw into Him, plug into Him, the one who wept over Jerusalem, the one who prayed with loud cries and tears, causes His tears to flow through those people. It's a measure of intimacy with God. They say something about the union and the fusion that nothing else can say. Peter was a man of tears.

Peter was chosen because he could be filled with the Holy Spirit such that in one day three thousand people were saved. Peter was chosen because he would become a Spirit-filled man. Peter was chosen because he would become a man repeatedly filled with the Holy Spirit.

In Acts 2 he was filled with the Holy Spirit.

In Acts 4:8.

"Then Peter, filled with the Holy Spirit, said to them ..."

In Acts 4:31b,

"And they were all filled with the Holy Spirit."

So twice Peter was filled with the Holy Spirit along with the rest. On another occasion, he was filled with the Holy Spirit as an individual. You could say that the Holy Spirit dwelt doubly on them all, and triply on Peter. That's one reason why Peter was chosen.

Peter was chosen because he would be so soaked with God that his shadow would have healing power. Peter was limitlessly filled with the Holy Spirit. His shadow healed the sick.

Peter was chosen because even when imprisoned for the Gospel, having been chained to one soldier on his right side and chained to another on the left expecting to face the firing squad the next day, he slept soundly, much at home with Jesus. After all, he was not in the hands of men; he was in the hands of Jesus. He was to be shot the next day but he slept soundly because he knew that after being shot on the following day, he would pass most assuredly into the presence of Jesus.

BACK MATTERS

If you have not yet received Jesus as your Lord and Saviour, I encourage you to receive Him. Here are some steps to help you,

ADMIT that you are a sinner by nature and by practice and that on your own you are without hope. Tell God you have personally sinned against Him in your thoughts, words and deeds. Confess your sins to Him, one after another in a sincere prayer. Do not leave out any sins that you can remember. Truly turn from your sinful ways and abandon them. If you stole, steal no more. If you have been committing adultery or fornication, stop it. God will not forgive you if you have no desire to stop sinning in all areas of your life, but if you are sincere, He will give you the power to stop sinning.

BELIEVE that Jesus Christ, who is God's Son, is the only Way, the only Truth and the only Life. Jesus said,

"I am the way, the truth and the life; no one comes to the Father, but by me" (John 14:6).

The Bible says,

> *"For there is one God, and there is one mediator between God and men, the man Christ Jesus, who gave himself as a ransom for all"* (1 Timothy 2:5-6).

> *"And there is salvation in no one else (apart from Jesus), for there is no other name under heaven given among men by which we must be saved"* (Acts 4:12).

> *But to all who received him, who believed in his name, he gave power to become children of God..."* (John 1:12).

BUT,

CONSIDER the cost of following Him. Jesus said that all who follow Him must deny themselves, and this includes selfish financial, social and other interests. He also wants His followers to take up their crosses and follow Him. Are you prepared to abandon your own interests daily for those of Christ? Are you prepared to be led in a new direction by Him? Are you prepared to suffer for Him and die for Him if need be? Jesus will have nothing to do with half-hearted people. His demands are total. He will only receive and forgive those who are prepared to follow Him AT ANY COST. Think about it and count the cost. If you are prepared to follow Him, come what may, then there is something to do.

INVITE Jesus to come into your heart and life. He says,

> *"Behold I stand at the door and knock. If anyone hears my voice and opens the door (to his heart and life), I will come in to him and eat with him, and he with me"* (Revelation 3:20).

Why don't you pray a prayer like the following one or one of your own construction as the Holy Spirit leads?

> *"Lord Jesus, I am a wretched, lost sinner who*
> *has sinned in thought, word and deed.*
> *Forgive all my sins and cleanse me.*
> *Receive me, Saviour and transform me*
> *into a child of God. Come into my heart*
> *now and give me eternal life right now. I*
> *will follow you at all costs, trusting the*
> *Holy Spirit to give me all the power I*
> *need."*

When you pray this prayer sincerely, Jesus answers at once and justifies you before God and makes you His child.

> *Please write to us (**ztfbooks@cmfionline.org**) and I will pray*
> *for you and help you as you go on with Jesus Christ.*

THANK YOU

For Reading This Book

If you have any question and/or need help, do not hesitate to contact us through **ztfbooks@cmfionline.org**. If the book has blessed you, then we would also be grateful if you leave a positive review at your favorite retailer.

ZTF BOOKS, through the Book Ministry of *Christian Missionary Fellowship International (CMFI)* offers a wide selection of best selling Christian books (in print, eBook & audiobook formats) on a broad spectrum of topics, including marriage & family, sexuality, practical spiritual warfare, Christian service, Christian leadership, and much more. Visit us at ztfbooks.com to learn more about our latest releases and special offers. And thank you for being a ZTF BOOK reader.

We invite you to connect with more from the author through social media (**cmfionline**) and/or ministry website (**ztfministry.org**), where we offer both on-ground and remote training courses (all year round) from basic to university level at the University of Prayer and Fasting (WUPF) and the School of Knowing and Serving God (SKSG). You are highly welcome to enrol at your soonest convenience. A FREE online Bible Course is also available.

We would like to recommend to you the next book in this series: *Laws Of Spiritual Success, Volume 1*

Success in the Christian life is defined as that which is approved by God, beginning in time and continuing in eternity. God views success first from the point of view of who we are and second from the point of view of what we do.

<u>All success is conditioned by prerequisites.</u> Here, the author highlights **12 essential laws that govern spiritual success**. These include

- clarity of direction,
- purpose and mission,
- the problems we face,
- God's provision for our success,
- believing God, others, and ourselves,
- forsaking sin, fleeing sin,
- etc.

Read this book and you will discover all the other laws that will certainly revolutionise your life.

Professor Zacharias Tanee Fomum was born in the flesh on 20th June 1945 and became born again on 13th June 1956. On 1st October 1966, He consecrated his life to the Lord Jesus and to His service, and was filled with the Holy Spirit on 24th October 1970. He was taken to be with the Lord on 14th March, 2009.

Pr Fomum was admitted to a first class in the Bachelor of Science degree, graduating as a prize winning student from Fourah Bay College in the University of Sierra Leone in October 1969. At the age of 28, he was awarded a Ph.D. in Organic Chemistry by the University of Makerere, Kampala in Uganda. In October 2005, he was awarded a Doctor of Science (D.Sc) by the University of Durham, Great Britain. This higher doctorate was in recognition of his distinct contributions to scientific knowledge through research. As a Professor of Organic Chemistry in the University of Yaoundé 1, Cameroon, Professor Fomum supervised or co-supervised more than 100 Master's Degree and Doctoral Degree theses and co-authored over 160 scientific articles in leading international journals. He considered Jesus Christ the Lord of Science ("For by Him all things were created..." – Colossians 1:16), and scientific research an act of obedience to God's command to "subdue the earth" (Genesis 1:28). He therefore made the Lord Jesus the Director of his research laboratory while he took the place of deputy director, and attributed his outstanding success as a scientist to Jesus' revelational leadership.

In more than 40 years of Christian ministry, Pr Fomum travelled extensively, preaching the Gospel, planting churches and training spiritual leaders. He made more than:

- 700 missionary journeys within Cameroon, which ranged from one day to three weeks in duration.
- 500 missionary journeys to more than 70 different nations in all the six continents. These ranged from two days to six weeks in duration.

By the time of his going to be with the Lord in 2009, he had preached in over 1000 localities in Cameroon, sent over 200 national missionaries into many localities in Cameroon and planted over 1300 churches in the various administrative provinces of Cameroon. At his base in Yaoundé, he planted and built a mega-church with his co-workers which grew to a steady membership of about 12,000. Pr Fomum was the founding team-leader of Christian Missionary Fellowship International (CMFI); an evangelism, soul-winning, disciple making, Church-planting and missionary-sending movement with more than 200 international missionaries and thousands of churches in 65 nations spread across Africa, Europe, the Americas, Asia and Oceania. In the course of their ministry, Pr Fomum and his team witnessed more than 10,000 recorded healing miracles performed by God in answer to prayer in the name of Jesus Christ. These miracles include instant healings of headaches, cancers, HIV/AIDS, blindness, deafness, dumbness, paralysis, madness, and new teeth and organs received.

Pr Fomum read the entire Bible more than 60 times, read more than 1350 books on the Christian faith and authored over 150 books to advance the Gospel of Jesus Christ. 5 million copies of these books are in circulation in 12 languages as well as 16 million gospel tracts in 17 languages.

Pr Fomum was a man who sought God. He spent between 15 minutes and six hours daily alone with God in what he called Daily Dynamic Encounters with God (DDEWG). During these DDEWG he read God's Word, meditated on it, listened to God's voice, heard God speak to him, recorded what God was saying to him and prayed it through. He thus had over 18,000 DDEWG. He also had over 60 periods of withdrawing to seek God alone for periods that ranged from 3 to 21 days (which he termed Retreats for Spiritual Progress). The time he spent seeking God slowly transformed him into a man who hungered, thirsted and panted after God. His unceasing heart cry was: "Oh, that I would have more of God!"

Pr Fomum was a man of prayer and a leading teacher on prayer in many churches and conferences around the world. He considered prayer to be the most important work that can be done for God and for man. He was a man of faith who believed that God answers prayer. He kept a record of his prayer requests and had over 50, 000 recorded answers to prayer in his prayer books. He carried out over 100 Prayer Walks of between five and forty-seven kilometres in towns and cities around the world. He and his team carried out over 57 Prayer Crusades (periods of forty days and nights during which at least eight hours are invested into prayer each day). They also carried out over 80 Prayer Sieges (times of near non-stop praying that ranges from 24 hours to 120 hours). He authored the Prayer Power Series, a 13-volume set of books on various aspects of prayer; Supplication, Fasting, Intercession and Spiritual Warfare. He started prayer chains, prayer rooms, prayer houses, national and continental prayer movements in Cameroon and other nations. He worked with leaders of local churches in India to disciple and train more than 2 million believers.

Pr Fomum also considered fasting as one of the weapons of Christian Spiritual Warfare. He carried out over 250 fasts ranging from three days to forty days, drinking only water or water supplemented with soluble vitamins. Called by the Lord to a distinct ministry of intercession, he pioneered fasting and prayer movements and led in battles against principalities and powers obstructing the progress of the Gospel and God's global purposes. He was enabled to carry out 3 supra – long fasts of between 52 and 70 days in his final years.

Pr Fomum chose a lifestyle of simplicity and "self- imposed poverty" in order to invest more funds into the critical work of evangelism, soul winning, church-planting and the building up of believers. Knowing the importance of money and its role in the battle to reach those without Christ with the glorious Gospel, he and his wife grew to investing 92.5% of their earned income from all sources (salaries, allowances, royalties and cash gifts) into the Gospel. They invested with the hope that, as they grew in the knowledge and the love of the Lord, and the perishing souls of people, they would one day invest 99% of their income into the Gospel.

He was married to Prisca Zei Fomum and they had seven children who are all involved in the work of the Gospel, some serving as missionaries. Prisca is a national and international minister, specializing in the winning and discipling of children to Jesus Christ. She also communicates and imparts the vision of ministry to children with a view to raising and building up ministers to them.

The Professor owed all that he was and all that God had done through him, to the unmerited favour and blessing of God and to his worldwide army of friends and co-workers. He considered himself nothing without them and the blessing of God; and would have amounted to nothing but for them. All praise and glory to Jesus Christ!

facebook.com/cmfionline

twitter.com/cmfionline

instagram.com/cmfionline

pinterest.com/cmfionline

youtube.com/cmfionline

ALSO BY Z.T. FOMUM

https://ztfbooks.com

THE CHRISTIAN WAY

1. The Way Of Life
2. The Way Of Obedience
3. The Way Of Discipleship
4. The Way Of Sanctification
5. The Way Of Christian Character
6. The Way Of Spiritual Power
7. The Way Of Christian Service
8. The Way Of Spiritual Warfare
9. The Way Of Suffering For Christ
10. The Way Of Victorious Praying
11. The Way Of Overcomers
12. The Way Of Spiritual Encouragement
13. The Way Of Loving The Lord

THE PRAYER POWER SERIES

1. The Way Of Victorious Praying
2. The Ministry Of Fasting
3. The Art Of Intercession
4. The Practice Of Intercession
5. Praying With Power
6. Moving God Through Prayer
7. Practical Spiritual Warfare Through Prayer
8. The Ministry Of Praise And Thanksgiving
9. Waiting On The Lord In Prayer

PRACTICAL HELPS FOR OVERCOMERS

SPIRITUAL LEADERSHIP

GOD, SEX AND YOU

OFF-SERIES

PRACTICAL HELPS IN SANCTIFICATION

17. The Salvation Of The Lord Jesus: Soul Winning
    (Vol. 3)

WOMEN OF THE GLORY

1. **The Secluded Worshipper**: The Life, Ministry,
   And Glorification Of The Prophetess Anna
2. **Unending Intimacy**: The Transformation, Choices
   And Overflow of Mary of Bethany
3. **Winning Love:** The rescue, development and
   fulfilment of Mary Magdalene
4. **Not Meant for Defeat**: The Rise, Battles, and
   Triumph of Queen Esther

ZTF COMPLETE WORKS

1. The School of Soul Winners and Soul Winning
2. Making Spiritual Progress (Volumes 1-4)
3. The Complete Works of Z.T.F on Holiness
   (Volume 1)
4. The Complete Works of Z.T.F on Basic Christian
   Doctrine
5. The Complete Works of Z.T.F on Marriage
   (Volume 1)
6. The Complete Works of Z.T.F on The Gospel
   Message (Volume 1)
7. The Complete Works of Z.T.F on Prayer (Volume 1)
8. The Complete Works of Z.T.F on Prayer (Volume 2)
9. The Complete Works of Z.T.F on Prayer (Volume 3)
10. The Complete Works of Z.T.F on Prayer (Volume 4)
11. The Complete Works of Z.T.F on Prayer (Volume 5)
12. The Complete Works of Z.T.F on Prayer (Volume 6)
13. The Complete Works of Z.T.F on Prayer (Volume 7)

SPECIAL SERIES

ZTF AUTO-BIOGRAPHIES

THE OVERTHROW OF PRINCIPALITIES

OTHER BOOKS

1. The Missionary as a Son
2. What Our Ministry is
3. Conserver la Moisson
4. Disciples of Jesus Christ to Make Disciples For Jesus Christ
5. The House Church in God's Eternal Purposes
6. Removing Obstacles Through Prayer and Fasting

DISTRIBUTORS OF ZTF BOOKS

These books can be obtained in French and English Language from any of the following distribution outlets:

EDITIONS DU LIVRE CHRETIEN (ELC)

- **Location:** Paris, France
- **Email:** editionlivrechretien@gmail.com
- **Phone:** +33 6 98 00 90 47

INTERNET

- **Location:** on all major online **eBook, Audiobook** and **print-on-demand** (paperback) retailers.
- **Email**: ztfbooks@cmfionline.org
- **Phone**: +47 454 12 804
- **Website**: ztfbooks.com

CPH YAOUNDE

- **Location:** Yaounde, Cameroon
- **Email:** editionsztf@gmail.com
- **Phone:** +237 74756559

ZTF LITERATURE AND MEDIA HOUSE

- **Location:** Lagos, Nigeria
- **Email:** zlmh@ztfministry.org
- **Phone:** +2348152163063

CPH BURUNDI

- **Location:** Bujumbura, Burundi
- **Email:** cph-burundi@ztfministry.org
- **Phone:** +257 79 97 72 75

CPH UGANDA

- **Location:** Kampala, Uganda
- **Email:** cph-uganda@ztfministry.org
- **Phone:** +256 785 619613

CPH SOUTH AFRICA

- **Location:** Johannesburg, RSA
- **Email:** tantohtantoh@yahoo.com
- **Phone:** +27 83 744 5682

NOTES

3. TIME SPENT ALONE WITH GOD IS WHAT MAKES A LEADER

1. Too bad for you.

5. PATHWAYS TO SPIRITUAL LEADERSHIP

1. ,3,4 Mimics pains of a woman at childbirth in the course of repeated delivery of babies who later turn out to be criminals.
2. Papa Solomon was brother Zach's father. A committed pastor of the Presbyterian Church of Cameroon.
3. Exclamation of pain.
4. An effervescence multivitamin tablets.
5. An effervescence multivitamin tablets.

8. WHY GOD CHOOSES PEOPLE TO BE LEADERS

1. A quarter in the city of Yaounde.

10. WHY GOD CHOOSES CERTAIN PEOPLE—GIDEON

1. Don't eat bitter kola any longer while fasting.

13. WHY GOD CHOOSES CERTAIN PEOPLE—THE FIRST THREE KINGS OF ISRAEL

1. They cannot measure u to him.

14. WHY GOD CHOOSES CERTAIN PEOPLE—PETER

1. High nines (in the French school system) Marks ranging from 9.7 – 9.9 on a total of 20 marks.